D0328853

THE
FEDERA
RATHOL

THE FEDERAL RATHOLE

DONALD LAMBRO

ARLINGTON HOUSE·PUBLISHERS
NEW ROCHELLE, NEW YORK

Copyright© 1975 by Donald Lambro.

All rights reserved. No portion of this book may be reproduced without written permission from the publisher except by a reviewer who may quote brief passages in connection with a review.

Manufactured in the United States of America.

Library of Congress Cataloging in Publication Data

Lambro, Donald.
    The Federal rathole.

    Includes index.
    1.   United States--Executive departments--Manage-
ment.   2.   United States--Appropriations and expenditures.   I.   Title.
JK421.L28   353   75-5669
ISBN 0-87000-294-5

For my Mother and Father
and for Jackie

Contents

Preface

Lord, the money we do spend on government, and it's not one bit better than the government we got for one-third the money 20 years ago.

WILL ROGERS

THIS BOOK WAS WRITTEN WITH THE FIRM belief that the American taxpayer, when provided with the facts about government spending, will wholeheartedly support a thorough housecleaning by Congress of wasteful, unneeded, outmoded, misdirected, and extravagant federal programs.

Comparatively little has been written about unnecessary and wasteful government spending, save for an infrequent newspaper or magazine article revealing the weird research and study grants that occasionally rise to the bureaucracy's surface. It is not the aim of this book to examine all of the government, nor to attempt to uncover every unneeded program. That would require an army of accountants and a far larger volume than this in which to recount each and every spending outrage. Instead, I have limited my inquiry to 50 specific programs or areas of government spending. Some are enormous, spending billions of dollars each year. Others are smaller, involving only a few hundred million annually. Some are simply examples of the hundreds of tiny federal programs that are sprinkled across the length and breadth of the government. The 50 cuts proposed in this book are really intended to represent a cross section of the total cuts that could be made in federal spending. They are

9

merely a starting point—should anyone wish to embark on a more ambitious expedition—from which further proposals to reduce spending can follow.

The total amount I suggest that could be saved is around $25 billion. It is the most accurate cost figure that could be calculated under the ground rules I set for myself. In most cases, the cost given for each program is the actual appropriation for the 1975 fiscal year. (A fiscal year is the government's accounting period which begins each July 1 and ends the following June 30.) Most of the costs listed are for a single fiscal year, except in cases where Congress specifically approved a program for more than one year and authorized funds covering the entire period. In these cases, authorizations are given in place of appropriations because Congress had not acted on the final spending figures at the time this book went to press. In a few cases, where no precise figures were available, I used the best estimates available.

One thing must be clearly understood from the beginning. I am not advocating that all 50 cuts be made in one fell swoop. The government's bureaucracy was built layer by layer. Unnecessary fat must be trimmed the same way. These programs must be gradually, sensibly phased out of existence. Some can be ended within a matter of months. Others would need a longer time in which to fulfill contractual obligations and to make an orderly, phased dismantling process possible. In many cases, certain essential activities within these programs must be retained or transferred to other agencies. All of this, obviously, would require time. But it can be done. Congress has the power to abolish any program it has enacted. It only needs the will, the determination, and the political courage to do so.

What I have attempted here is to draw up a summary of the arguments against each program and to construct each case for its dissolution. My information, and many of my ideas, come from numerous sources, including conversations with officials in various departments and agencies, government reports, speeches, articles, and congressional testimony and debate.

There has perhaps been too great a tendency within the media to focus on social problems while looking to Washington as the pre-eminent solution to those problems. Journalists have all but ignored vast waste in government, which is often as much a burden to taxpayers as some of the very social and economic ills that have consumed the media's attention.

Perhaps a healthy dose of skepticism, aimed at government, is needed. Government programs do not always work, are not always worth continuing, and are not immune to massive abuse. Occasionally, a congressional committee will focus on some eyesore of government waste needing reform and the media will duly report the event. Yet little independent aggressive probing into waste and duplication has been evident. The media, it seems to me, tend to think too much in terms of new government programs—as does Congress—and never in terms of exploring whether old ones should be abolished. The purpose of this book is to focus attention on the subject of waste in government, to move us a little closer to the day when it will become the number-one priority for both social and economic reform.

DONALD LAMBRO
Washington, D.C.

Introduction

EACH WEEKLY PAYCHECK STUB IS A CONSTANT and painful reminder to the American taxpayer that Washington has gone berserk.

Annual federal budget requests are now over $349 billion and climbing, with the fiscal 1977 budget conservatively projected to hit $393 billion. The gross federal debt reached $504 billion by the end of 1974 and was estimated to go over $605 billion by the end of the 1976 fiscal year. Interest on the debt is costing taxpayers over $29 billion a year and is estimated to rise to $36 billion annually by June 30, 1976. Between 1970 and 1974 the government ran up deficits of $68 billion, but Treasury Secretary William Simon predicts that in 1975 alone the government will have to borrow $79 billion to pay its mounting bills. Under President Ford's proposed fiscal 1976 budget, government spending will race upward to nearly $1 billion a day. Meanwhile, the average taxpayer must work four full months each year just to pay his total federal, state and local taxes. And there is no end in sight.

There are an estimated 81 million tax returns filed by taxpayers in America. It is they who provide most of the tax dollars that finance the federal government. Out of total federal tax revenues of $268.9 billion for the fiscal year period ending June 30, 1974, corporations provided over $41.8 billion while total individual taxes were over $142.7 billion. Even if corporate taxes were doubled—as some in Congress apparently would like—revenues still wouldn't approach anywhere near what individual taxpayers give their government. Meanwhile, despite what congressmen and bureaucrats may say, federal taxes are going up. The Social Security tax rate rose from 5.2 percent to 5.85 percent in 1973, and there have been increases in the base income on which the tax is levied in 1973, 1974 and 1975. In fact, all federal taxes have risen more rapidly than any other cost in the average American family's budget in the past half dozen years.

Figures compiled by the U. S. Chamber of Commerce show that spending by local, state, and federal governments in 1930 was about 10 percent of personal income. In 1940 it reached 20 percent. In 1970 the amount was 36 percent. Today total government spending is close to 40 percent of personal income. We've reached a point where the average worker must toil from January 1 until May 1 to earn enough money to pay all his taxes. According to computations by Tax Foundation, Inc., the average American taxpayer must work more than two and a half hours a day every work week to pay all of his federal, state, and local taxes. The inexorable trend in government is to accumulate more and more tax revenue so as to increase public spending and reduce private spending. The result is that it takes the average American longer and longer to pay his share of government's cost before he can begin working for himself.

Administrations come and go pledging to reduce the runaway costs of big government. Some even produce exciting rhetoric about slashing personnel, cutting waste, and dismantling long-forgotten vestiges of the federal behemoth. But no reductions of any major substance have ever been made. For all the cost-cutting rhetoric of the Nixon administration, President Nixon was the biggest deficit-spender of any President since World War II. Nixon, from fiscal 1970 through fiscal 1974, ran up deficits of $2.8 billion, $23 billion, $23.2 billion, $14.3 billion, and $4.7 billion, respectively.

One of the central tenets of conservatives has been to reduce the size and influence of the federal bureaucracy in an effort to cut down spending and thereby to ease the taxpayer's burden and curb inflation. Yet, even among conservatives in Congress, very little beyond emotional appeals to fiscal responsibility and dire predictions of doom and gloom is heard. Liberals have been far more aggressive in advancing their goals of government expansion. A plan once advanced by Democrats simply to abolish tax exemptions and loopholes and then review them one by one to see if they were needed and should be retained, comes most notably to mind as an example of their daring in pursuing their own ideological visions. But could—would—anyone in Congress similarly propose that 100 government agencies not be funded in the next budget request until each and every one of them had met a rigorous test of need? Yet that may be the only way a scrupulous review of wasteful government spending can ever be achieved.

In advancing the reasons for his own meager and largely unsuccessful efforts to reduce extravagant federal spending, President Nixon once expressed the notion that Congress was incapable of taking such actions because it was captive to too many special interests. He was only partly right, of course, because the President is also in many ways, though to a lesser degree, a prisoner of interest groups, both inside and outside government. It must be noted in connection with this that the loudest voices among them are those whose very jobs are being threatened—the bureaucrats themselves.

Whenever fiscal conservatives venture forth to debate government spending, they are inevitably met with the question, "Yes, but where would you begin to cut back?" It is unfortunate that in all the encounters conservatives have had with liberals over the issue of waste in government, they have seldom been able to recite in detail the obvious federal tentacles that could be chopped off without the slightest ho-hum from the American taxpayer. But ask the big government protagonist where he would like to see a broader federal involvement in the lives of Americans and he'll regurgitate an unending list of all sorts of good deeds he would like to see accomplished.

Perhaps there are many areas where good things can be wrought by government on problems that have long plagued our nation. And conservatives might very well support certain proposals if rampant federal spending could first be brought under control and unneeded programs trimmed from the annual budget. But new proposals are not the concern of this book.

What is irrefutable in the mind of this conservative is that there is rampant waste, duplication, and squandering of hard-earned taxes throughout the federal government. An examination of hundreds of boards, departments, agencies, commissions, councils, committees, and other federal programs shows there is a plethora of fat to be trimmed. What I have tried to do in this book is to identify the most obvious areas where specific programs are not working, or are duplicating the work of other programs, or where their purposes are vague and almost totally lacking in priority.

In most of the cases, the choices were not difficult to make. Many programs seem almost to beg to be abolished. For some, where the overall purpose behind a program sounds worthwhile, the decisions were not as easily arrived at, though upon closer examination I found that the programs were not achieving anywhere near their desired goals. In still others, there are parts of programs that had to be continued but could be merged with other agencies whose bloated staffs could easily handle the increased workload. In still other programs I had one overriding criterion for termination: we can't afford it. In the case of revenue sharing—by far the biggest spending program of my 50 proposed cuts—it wasn't very hard to arrive at that decision as the Treasury Department sold billions of dollars in short-term bills, paying almost 10 percent interest, in order to raise enough money to pay its bills.

The fact that I chose to limit myself to 50 spending items doesn't mean there aren't 50 more, even 100 more. Quite frankly, 50 was a totally arbitrary figure on my part. It had a nice solid ring to it and I had to stop somewhere. And, too, government programs have a tendency to overwhelm to the point of numbness.

Moreover, my inquiries were limited to agencies or entire programs of government and not to isolated grants, research projects, contracts, or other selected spending activities. The record of the federal government is swamped with examples of such mystifying spending schemes: The Bedouins were given $17,000 for a dry-cleaning plant to clean their djellabas. We studied the smell of perspiration from Australian aborigines for a mere $70,000. We've also spent $15,000 to study Yugoslavian lizards, $71,000 to compile a history of comic books, $5,000 to analyze violin varnish, $19,300 to determine why children fall off tricycles, and $375,000 for the Pentagon to study Frisbees. And there are extravagances to satisfy the personal whims of bureaucrats who are supposed to be the people's servants. Attorney General William Saxbe ripped out the carpeting in his predecessor's office because he did not like the color. New carpeting and a new decor to go with it ripped off taxpayers for $79,500.

Postmaster General E. T. Klassen installed a new $800 marble-topped lavatory as part of his elaborate $149,100 office refurbishing. The government is spending $13 million a year on chauffer-driven limousines for government officials; another $13.9 million a year is being spent to maintain 300 military golf courses in 19 foreign countries and the United States; and face lifts, breast enlargement operations and other types of cosmetic surgery are being routinely performed without charge on wives of military personnel in military medical centers. Examples of waste and extravagance like these would themselves fill a book. I chose instead to approach the matter on a program-by-program basis. If spending is to be substantially reduced and waste curbed, then government itself has to be trimmed. That means whole agencies and programs. Offices have to be closed down. Bureaucrats must be returned to the private sector where they can produce revenue rather than spend it.

Cutting back government also requires destroying a myth—that most of the federal budget is "uncontrollable," cemented into place by Congress, and neither heaven nor hell can move it. In testimony before the Senate Budget Committee, Roy Ash, director of the Office of Management and Budget, argued that out of the entire fiscal 1975 budget about $92.2 billion could be labeled discretionary as opposed to $225 billion that he termed "mandatory spending." Ash said that if you removed from the discretionary column some $57.1 billion in defense spending, that left $35.1 billion in nondefense costs, or about 11 percent of the total budget. Housing subsidies, farm supports, Social Security, food stamps, Medicare and Medicaid, and veterans benefits are just a few of the monstrous programs that he places in the uncontrollable corner. The fact is that what Congress has granted, Congress can take away or whittle down. I do not know whether Mr. Ash would place the 50 programs in this book on his list of uncontrollables. Yet all of them can be dissolved by acts of Congress. The laws can be amended. There is nothing sacrosanct about a government program. Reasonable men, convinced of the need for government frugality, can adopt a budget that will reduce spending. When faced with rising debts and a mounting financial crisis, it is reasonable to expect that a business or a family will sharply reduce its outlays. In that situation, what may have been deemed essential no longer is so. Government can do the same.

There are a number of reasons why cutting down on government spending would be good for America. First, it could lead to a true reform of our tax structure through which Americans could be given some genuine tax reductions. Second, it would help the economy by reducing government borrowing and thus leave more capital in the private sector for business investment and development. Treasury Secretary William Simon has stated that if the government could maintain, on average, a budget surplus equal to even one-half percent of the gross national product, "we would add about three percent to the flow of savings available to the private sector." But third, and foremost, reduced spending would help to curb inflation.

There are liberals in Congress who will argue with their last dying breath that deficit spending does not contribute to inflation. To concede that it does would of course mean they would have to narrow their spending programs severely within the confines of a balanced budget. Perish the thought.

But a comparison of federal budgets over the past 26 years—from 1948 to 1973—shows there is an underlying relationship between inflation and deficits. In fact, the figures show clearly that above-average rates of inflation appear when the budget runs a sizable deficit, and below-average inflation rates follow consistently sizable budget surpluses.

Secretary Simon noted that except for two unique fiscal years in 1950-51 and 1973-74, when commodity inflation had an extraordinary impact on prices, "The relationship strongly supports the general notion that budget deficits are inflationary and budget surpluses are not inflationary."

It has also become increasingly evident that federal loan or loan-guarantee programs have significantly fed inflation by draining needed capital from the private money markets, thus contributing to tighter money supply and rising interest rates. In fact, there is considerable evidence that federally authorized borrowing agencies are probably as much a factor in pushing inflation upward as are budget deficits. Even so, Congress seems more than ever disposed to establishing new loan programs as a solution to almost any national ill. Borrowing by various federal agencies grew between 1969 and 1974 from $4.3 billion to $47.2 billion. The list of agencies authorized to borrow capital includes the Federal Financing Bank, the Federal Home Loan banks, the Federal National Mortgage Association, the Export-Import Bank, the Postal Service Fund, the Rural Electrification and Telephone revolving fund, the Federal Home Loan Mortgage Corporation, the Farm Credit Administration, and the

Student Loan Marketing Association. If Congress truly wanted to do something about soaring interest rates and inflation it should reexamine the lending agencies it has established, agencies which remove billions of dollars each year from the private sector.

The centrifugal force with which federal spending, and thus inflation, is being propelled is almost impossible to comprehend. Here's one way to put it into sharper focus: It took America 185 years for its government to hit the $100-billion level in federal spending, only nine additional years after that to reach $200 billion and just four years later to reach the present $300-billion-plus mark.

In the 10-year period from 1955 to 1965 federal spending rose at about a six percent annual rate. From 1965 to 1974 federal spending was propelled to a 10 percent annual rate of growth. Rapid spending increases have resulted in massive deficits, which in turn have fed demands and thus inflation.

Who feeds government spending? Congress is the prime culprit. The bureaucracy is another. Bureaucrats and lawmakers alike have retrieved their own rewards for the part they've played in bloating the bureaucracy.

It is unfortunate, yet true, that many senators and congressmen believe their political careers will rise or fall in large measure on the number of bills they introduce and the programs they enact. The more bills they can maneuver through Congress and get signed into law, the higher they believe their stock will rise among their constituencies, the media, and their colleagues. The more ambitious the spending program, the more reward received.

On the other hand, little national attention is ever given to those members who come to Congress vowing to vote against excessive spending. Many of them are regarded as congressional anachronisms by the general media and their tribulations against excessive spending usually go unnoticed—although, it must be admitted, many fiscal conservatives possess little flair and often present their case very poorly. Today, the senator or congressman who runs for reelection boasting that he voted against spending programs because the government was in debt and couldn't afford them, seems, more than ever, to be falling behind the liberal who promises to support a cornucopia of new programs supposedly to "help the people."

The bureaucrats who run these programs are also an integral part of the spending syndrome. For under the unspoken rules of the game, they can never seek smaller budgets for their agencies or try to make economies to reduce costs. As one bureaucrat confessed publicly: "Because the deadline for federal spending in each fiscal year is June 30, the result is affectionately referred to as June buying. The federal guy funds all the half-baked ideas that have been on the back burner all year. If his budget is not spent, it is logically inconsistent to ask for more. But worse, there's the chance of getting less. In this town, it is a mark of failure to administer a program whose budget is going down. Budgets are like sales curves: they should go up over the years. A sharp increase indicates a hot program, one viewed as growth stock in the government."

Obviously, if you want to succeed in Washington, you must build up your program, hire more personnel, issue more contracts, draw up new guidelines, and plead with Congress that more money is needed if Congress's intent is to be faithfully carried out. And the crush of bureaucratic work is literally staggering to behold. According to the General Accounting Office, federal paperwork now crams nearly 30 million cubic feet of space and costs an estimated $15 billion a year to handle. Placed back to back, the federal files would stretch the 5,500 miles from Washington to Cairo—and are forever growing. (Tibet or bust!)

The total cost of government and its burgeoning debt each year become less and less meaningful for the average American, who is unmoved by the sheer enormity of the figures. None of the figures really means very much to the average taxpayer; he simply has no way economically to relate to monster totals other than through their component parts. That is, how much does each department or agency or program cost? And what is it doing for me? The taxpayer looks at the withholding sum on his paycheck, sees that the weeks he must work to pay his due to the federal government are becoming depressingly longer, and begins—one prays—to ask if there will be an end to programs that seem to fulfill little need and yet expend enormous sums of money. His money. One hopes for the day when taxpayers, and more congressmen, will begin asking, "Do we need this program?"

Yet within Congress there continues to be an almost religious commitment to dream up federal programs for every conceivable national ill. One wonders at times whether we have evolved into a system of government in which 435 representatives and 100 senators are being paid $42,500 a year primarily to think up ways to spend our money. And the ideas, which become spending programs, never cease. Birch Bayh, Democratic senator from Indiana, introduced—and Congress enacted—a bill that coughed up over $10 million a year to build shelters across the country to house runaway youths (which I discuss in a later chapter). Indiana's other Democratic senator, Vance Hartke, once relieved himself of an idea that would expend hundreds of millions of dollars over several years to develop a high-speed rail service that would flash passengers between New York and Washington in half the time it now takes. One immediately wonders— especially one who prefers the contemplative pace of train travel—why would anyone want to travel that fast and why should the federal government finance such a pipedream. Unfortunately, pipedreams in Congress become laws. Thousands of them are introduced each year.

There is nothing that comes closer to achieving immortality than a federal program. Once enacted, it goes on seemingly forever, its funds appropriated almost automatically each year, its original rationale for being often all but forgotten.

I possess no illusions that Congress, as it is presently constituted, will make any of these cuts in the foreseeable future. Congress is a miasma of competing interest blocs and every member has his pet programs that he will fight like hell to defend, although, as the reader will find out, proponents of these programs often provide the best arguments for their demise.

Here, however, is a case-by-case argument for 50 cuts in government spending. Henceforth, let no one say that conservatives talk about cutting back on the size of government but are incapable of pointing to exactly where they would wield the axe. Perhaps these modest suggestions for fiscal retrenchment, and the arguments made for each, will be of some help in firing up the American taxpayer to urge a halt to wasteful government spending. I hope so. For it is clear the budgetary blade can be surgically applied across the entire body of government and the treatment should read: "Cut to the bone."

1

1,250 Federal Advisory Boards, Committees, Commissions, and Councils

$75 Million

THE FEDERAL GOVERNMENT IS LITERALLY drenched in advisory committees—1,250 of them at last count.*

An estimated 24,000 private and public citizens sit on these so-called advisory panels and commissions, which are fueled and run by an assigned government staff of more than 4,000 employees. The estimated annual cost to taxpayers—more than $75 million.

Often referred to as the "fifth arm of government," the panels were the object of a rather weak attempt by Congress in late 1972 to exert some control over their almost cancerous growth. Unfortunately, there is little indication thus far that their numbers have been appreciably reduced.

The first-known federal advisory committee was used by George

---

*An alphabetical list of all 1,250 is provided in Appendix I.

Washington to assist him in dealing with the Whisky Rebellion. Like everything else in government, the committees grew—so large and so fast that by 1970, when congressional concern over their population began to peak, no one in government had the slightest idea how many there were, who served on them, and what they cost to operate.

A congressional study found that every nook and cranny of government was teeming with them and that their numbers were growing with each passing year. It seemed that every new or renewed program mandated by Congress required the establishment of a new advisory committee. Whenever a problem cried out for solution, Presidents invariably established a blue-ribbon commission to look into the matter and issue a report. As government grew and became more and more remote from the people, the routine proposal was to bring in the private sector via an advisory role. It gave at least the appearance of government consulting its people before making substantive decisions.

Thus, today there is a committee for almost any subject the mind of man can conceive. There are, for example, an Advisory Panel for Anthropology, one for foot-and-mouth disease, a National Peanut Advisory Committee, an advisory panel on raisins, a Plant Variety Protection Board, a National Board for the Promotion of Rifle Practice, a Waterfowl Advisory Committee, at least two review committees on contraceptives, one on antiperspirants, a Committee for the Recovery of Archaeological Remains, and an advisory committee for every national forest in America. Yes, there is even a review committee on laxatives.

There are also a Social Problems Research Review Committee (whatever that is), a Women's Advisory Committee on Aviation, a Census Advisory Committee on Privacy and Confidentiality, a Theatre Advisory Panel, a Dance Advisory Panel, a Personality Research Review Committee, and a Panel on Review of Sunburn Treatment. And what in heaven's name would the government do without the now infamous Board of Tea Tasters! President Nixon suggested dumping their bag in a cost-cutting speech in 1970 but they're still brewing and tasting. Nixon, on February 26 of that year, went on television to seek support for his alleged cost-cutting efforts, citing the federal tea tasters as a prime example of waste in government. "At one time in the dim past," he said, "there may have been good reason for such special taste tests; but that reason no longer exists. Nevertheless, a separate tea-tasting board has gone right along, at the taxpayer's expense, because nobody up to now took the trouble to take a hard look at why it

24

was in existence."

As of this writing, that board still exists, tea-tasting at the taxpayer's expense. It requested $178,250 for its fiscal 1974 budget. No action was ever taken by the administration to eliminate tea tasting as a tax-supported government program. Every budget that was sent to Congress since Nixon's impassioned television plea for fiscal restraint contained a request for funds to pay the salaries and expenses of the six official tea tasters making up the board. Not only that, but funds were also requested for a United States Board of Tea Appeals. Imagine, if a tea importer didn't like the verdict of the official tea taster, he could ask the appeals board for another chance. After that, the appeals board was authorized to call in independent consultants to settle any continuing dispute.

The board offsets its costs through a small fee of 3.5 cents per hundredweight charged to tea importers, but those fees cover only about a quarter of the cost. The taxpayers, in other words, are left holding the bag.

Many of these committees, according to congressional testimony and government reports, haven't met for years. Often, when they do, it is in secret sessions, closed to the public they are supposed to represent. Moreover, it is almost impossible to find out when these meetings occur or what was discussed, since transcripts are seldom kept.

Who serves on these committees? Well, for one thing government sees that it is well represented on its own advisory boards. The Defense Department has more representatives on advisory committees than any other agency—713. The University of California has more representatives than any other institution of higher learning, 374, followed by Harvard, 130, and Columbia, 108. Corporations with large numbers of representatives on these panels include RCA, 93; ITT, 92; Communications Satellite Corporation (a quasi-government corporation), 81; and General Electric, 79. Oil companies also have large representations as do the AFL-CIO and its labor affiliates, which held at least 226 separate positions at last count.

Scanning the massive 995-page index prepared by the Library of Congress Research Service in 1973, which listed the committees and their members, overwhelming duplication becomes painfully apparent. There were, for example, at least four committees on women's rights: the Citizens Advisory Council on the Status of Women; the President's

Study Group on Careers for Women; the Interdepartmental Committee on the Status of Women, and the Task Force on Women's Rights and Representatives.

Like almost everything else in government, advisory committees are virtually immortal. The Business Advisory Council on Federal Reports set up under Franklin D. Roosevelt is alive and well. President Truman's National Petroleum Council still prospers.

Invariably, when one discusses advisory committees, the Commission on Standardization of Screw Threads—now the Interdepartmental Screw Thread Committee—raises its ugly head as the clearest example of government longevity in all its glory. The commission was organized in 1918 with a promise by its proponents that it would need only one year to complete its study and then be gone. But it was continued, for reasons long since forgotten, for three years. And in 1922 there was still another three-year extension. The commission had spent $150,000 in its first eight years of existence. And on and on it went until today it is all but a permanent fixture of the bureaucracy.

Such examples are of course heavily laced throughout the maze of advisory committees, many of which are directed by Congress or the President to study some problem and issue a report, which few people will ever read, and recommendations, which fewer still will ever follow. The Commission on Obscenity and Pornography produced a report that cost $1.8 million and that was publicly disavowed by the White House before its submission. The National Commission on the Causes and Prevention of Violence spent $1.3 million on its report. (The money would have been better spent training our police and improving our court systems.) The National Commission on Urban Problems spent $1.5 million to come up with a report that President Johnson refused to accept.

When you consider all the wasteful things the government spends money on, encouraging physical fitness and athletic activity is certainly a worthwhile endeavor. But there is little or no evidence that the millions of dollars the President's Council on Physical Fitness and Sports has spent have in fact improved the physical fitness of Americans in any measurable way. This council comes under the Department of Health, Education and Welfare's Office of Human Development and has been operating under one name or another since 1956. Its half-million-dollar-plus budget ($525,000) goes primarily for producing public service advertising to promote physical fitness and sports activities, for distributing

26

literature, and for providing an awards program for children and adults. Physical fitness and athletics are, and should remain, private undertakings, to be promoted by concerned and involved individuals and organizations and not the federal government.

Other advisory panels likewise pull down tremendous budgets. The Commission on the Review of the National Policy Toward Gambling received for fiscal year 1975 an appropriation of $1 million for salaries and expenses. The Advisory Commission on Intergovernmental Relations was funded in 1975-76 to the tune of $1,075,000 for salaries and expenses.

In 1973 legislation was enacted to deal with this incredible birth rate in committees by—you guessed it—establishing another committee. Public law 92-463 created the Supreme Allied Commander of government committees within the Office of Management and Budget (OMB)—the Committee Management Secretariat, "responsible for all matters relating to advisory committees." It was ordered, among other things, to conduct a comprehensive review of every committee to determine which were needed, where mergers could be sensibly made to end duplication, and where some could be abolished.

In June 1974, OMB issued a report proudly boasting that of the 1,439 committees that had been in existence by the end of 1972, 390 committees had been abolished by December 1973. However, during this same trimming-down period, 216 new committees had been created, 24 of them by acts of Congress. Thus, there had been a net decrease of only 174 committees.

These committees, boards, commissions, councils, review panels, whatever you call them, have become, in the words of Sen. Lee Metcalf (D.-Mont.), a "headless monster." Congressional investigators who have been studying these committees for years privately admit that 90 percent of them could be abolished tomorrow without so much as a ripple in the machinery of government.

No doubt there are some on the list—those crucial to the nation's defense and the health of its citizens—that have made some worthwhile contributions. If so, perhaps some exceptions should be made under a stern evaluation by OMB. But the evidence is abundantly clear that an arm of government evolved where none was ever intended. If government needs advisory experts, it should hire them as situations arise. It can contract for such services when necessary. If the problem is a legitimately long-range one, taxpayers expect their taxes to pay the cost of hiring the best brains available to grapple with it on a full-time basis. The committees should be abolished.

2

Federal Film-Making and Audio Programs

$150 Million

THERE IS NO OTHER AREA IN THE ENTIRE government that is as swamped with duplication as this one; no other more appallingly wasteful than this, as millions of dollars are spent for government films and recordings, most of which few taxpayers will ever see or hear.

Since World War I, the government has made an estimated 100,000 films on every subject from toothbrushes to soybeans—an average of 2,000 films a year. Bureaucrats say even this figure may be well short of the actual number. To this day, no one in the government knows precisely how many films are actually being made each year or the specific total cost of all this celluloid to the American taxpayer.

According to a little-noticed report issued by the White House Office of Telecommunications in February 1974, the government spent at least $375 million in 1972 to produce and distribute films, photographs, and

29

an assortment of recorded programs and audio services. These programs covered a wide range of subjects and were produced by government employees working out of at least 653 federal facilities scattered throughout the government.

Some of these audiovisual costs include the Voice of America; scientific, space, and weapons testing analysis; and other experimental programs. Obviously, legitimate film and audio work for weapons testing, experimental analysis, and certain intelligence-gathering and propaganda activities (operated by the Central Intelligence Agency and the U. S. Information Agency) should be maintained (although the military is also filled with wasteful and costly film facilities that too often are used primarily for public relations and have no actual defense-related needs).

Of the $375 million spent annually by 15 major federal agencies examined by the Office of Telecommunications, at least $150 million is spent solely on audiovisual activities involved in the "communications of messages to audiences," as opposed to testing, analysis and reference activities, and the overseas work of the VOA. Although I believe the $150-million figure represents at best a conservative estimate, it is the best figure that anyone in the government has come up with for the type of government spending that has to be placed on the lowest rung of the priority ladder.

The report by the Office of Telecommunications found rampant waste and duplication. For example, it revealed that there was "little or no coordination of the plans of departments and component agencies for new audio-visual equipment and facilities. . . . At least two of the largest audiovisual production and processing facilities in the government are operating at or below 50 percent capacity."

Among its recommendations: "Federal departments and agencies should phase out all in-house motion picture processing facilities except (1) those which support time critical audiovisual documentation in remote locations such as weapons test sites, and (2) those which support military combat or intelligence operations."

Interestingly, of the 653 facilities identified by the study, 479 were still photographic operations or, in a few instances, audio facilities. Ninety percent of these still photo labs were in the Defense Department—many of them clustered around Washington, D. C., Norfolk, Va., and Southern California—which fact, the report said (in an extraordinary understatement), would "suggest that consolidation may be in order." Of the remaining 174 facilities, 41 were capable of processing motion-picture films but were engaged in no productions. All but one of the 41 were in the Defense Department. The remaining 133 facilities that were engaged in both videotape and motion-picture production included 52 in the Veterans Administration; 10 in the Transportation Department; 46 in Defense; 10 in Health, Education and Welfare; and 4 in the National Aeronautics and Space Administration.

The report also found that in a review of 16 different federal agency film catalogs, "the same subjects seem to appear regularly." During 1972, the Army, Navy, Air Force, and USIA acquired some 20,000 films representing 830 titles at a cost of $4 million. The report confessed that it attempted to estimate the extent of overlap in such films but that "this turned out to be an all but impossible task."

Even more difficult to grasp is the incredible number of films and other audiovisual print purchases by other government agencies. There are 3,309 titles alone in the U. S. Air Force catalog, 65 percent of them produced by the Air Force. "The other 35 percent were produced elsewhere and are probably listed several times in government catalogs," the report said. For example, a film produced jointly by the National Aeronautics and Space Administration (NASA) and the Bureau of Public Roads, entitled "Automobile Tire Hydroplaning—What Happens," is listed in at least five different government catalogs. On the subject of driving safety, the Air Force has produced 11 films since 1960, four of which were released in 1972. During the same period, the Department of Health, Education and Welfare made two films on the same subject, while the Army, NASA, and the Transportation Department also produced one film each on driving safety.

In a typical government hit-them-over-the-head approach, the study gives the government's rationale for having this many films on the same subject: ". . . you can't show the same one twice to the same audience with any effect; a barrage of films is needed to have an impact over a period of time." The government now has in stock an estimated 1.4 million film prints that cover 58,000 separate titles.

One Republican congressman, Barry Goldwater, Jr. of California, made what in many respects is a more thorough inquiry into the government's film activities. Unfortunately, the 66-page report Goldwater issued on his findings received scant attention from the news media.

The vast majority of audiovisual materials, Goldwater found, were being produced by 13 major agencies, including Agriculture, Defense, HEW, the USIA, the Atomic Energy Commission, the Environmental Protection Agency, and the Interior and Justice Departments. The National Audio-Visual Center of the National Archives, in a separate inventory it undertook, listed a total of 45 separate agencies and their subdivisions that produce films and other audiovisual materials. Within these 45 units of government, 1,461 *key* employees were identified in jobs overseeing film-making for Uncle Sam. As we have seen, the largest expenditure on government films is made by the Defense Department, which in fiscal 1972 alone spent $27.8 million for the salaries of 1,530 audiovisual employees (which averages out to $18,122.16 per employee), according to Goldwater's investigation.

Goldwater found that rather than going to the private sector to contract for such films, "this government is doing the majority of work itself while literally thousands of professionals are unemployed and millions of dollars in private equipment and facilities are not being utilized." He also found that the Defense Department alone had more than $289.8 million worth of film equipment spread out over 2,000 military facilities. This is of course another example of the government going into business for itself on a massive scale to the detriment of a private industry (film-making), which could no doubt do the job more efficiently and more cheaply.

Needless to say, throughout the government's film extravaganza the right hand knows not what the left hand is doing, and rampant duplication of film facilities, staff, and equipment is the result. Six of the seven major agencies within the sprawling HEW bureaucracy, for example, have their own facilities and equipment.

Here are some choice examples of what your government is doing for you in the film business:

Your Teeth Are in Your Hands is a $35,000 film series made by the U. S. Navy to instruct recruits how to care for their teeth.

In *Mulligan Stew* the Agriculture Department spent $300,000 to teach children about good nutrition.

HEW made *America on the Rocks*, a $375,000 film which—brace yourself—discovered that alcoholism is a middle-class problem.

In *Games*, the U. S. Army spent $60,000 to explore racism.

How to Succeed with Brunettes is part of a $64,000 film series by the Navy on etiquette, not for enlisted men, but for officers. This flick inculcates the art of assisting milady with her coat while another epic, *Blondes Prefer Gentlemen*, teaches officers how to maneuver suavely through a dinner party.

The government—again, agencies going off on their own with little knowledge of what the other is doing—has produced around 585 dental films in what would appear to be a chronic oral fixation by Washington. Most of the 585 were made by the Veterans Administration. At least 12 of the films tell how to brush your teeth. An additional 14 film classics will tell you everything you have ever wanted to know (but were afraid to ask) about venereal disease. The Navy made one called *The Return of Count Spirochete.*

Newsman Mike Wallace explored government film-making on the CBS program "60 Minutes" and concluded: "Nobody argues about the need for warning young recruits about the dangers of venereal disease, but do we need 14 films about it? And there is duplication and repetition not only in toothbrushing and VD but in environment and drugs and pollution."

The Agriculture Department, the oldest government film-maker on the Potomac, has been grinding out movies for 50 years. And for years it has been churning out television programs on such subjects as good nutrition, often using Agriculture employees or hired actors who appear to be reporters getting out the government line.

"Various government departments," Wallace found, "have been making and distributing short film clips that look like news stories. The television stations get free programming; the government gets its message out; the viewer gets persuasion—packaged as news."

As with all propaganda about the government's own activities, failure is usually hidden from the public, or at least never reported through its "public information" outlets. During the Johnson administration, at the height of the antipoverty war, the Office of Economic Opportunity paid $175,000 for a film produced by Charles Guggenheim about an OEO-sponsored community law-enforcement project that failed. The film, which showed that failure, was junked by OEO. In another instance, the Navy paid out $46,000 for a movie about Chicanos called *Red, White, Blue and Brown.* Because the film criticized government treatment of Chicanos, the commissioned movie was never released.

And of course government bureaucrats are always eager to glorify their own accomplishments. This has been done in thousands of self-serving films by departments and agencies interested only in blowing their own horn. Toward this end, HEW Secretary Elliot Richardson commissioned a film in 1972 to peddle the agency's story at a cost of $125,000. Fortunately, when Caspar Weinberger took over HEW he refused to release *Toward Freedom*, calling it "an unnecessary, . . . wasteful expenditure."

Unbelievable as it may sound, no one in any official capacity knows exactly how much film-making is really going on. No master list of government films exists; no single watchdog agency is charged with regulating this out-of-control desire to sell Washington to the taxpayers via the silver screen.

Even when you get down to the lower echelons of government and talk to those who are supposed to be in charge of their own film-making facilities, there is no one who can tell you what is going on. Mike Wallace talked with Maurice McDonald, chief of HEW's Audio-Visual Department, and hit a blank wall:

Wallace: Do you know how many films you make?

McDonald: No, I can't give you an exact answer.

Wallace: Do you know how many films that you've made in the last two years?

McDonald: I haven't done a count on them.

Wallace: Do you know where I would go to get that list? Is there a list?

McDonald: There is no list.

The Office of Telecommunications, in its report, seemed similarly exasperated at its inability to obtain needed data: "Practically all of these studies are hampered by the same lack of consistent data with which to affirm or deny that there is more (or less) being produced in-house, that there are more (or fewer) facilities, that consolidation is (or is not) taking place, and that agencies do (or do not) act in ignorance of what other agencies are doing."

Weinberger, in an interview with CBS, agreed with Wallace that throughout the government "nobody knows who is doing what film for whom at what cost." Confessed Weinberger, "We tried at the Office of Management and Budget to get each department to furnish us that specific kind of information and invariably the reply came back that the information systems weren't able to produce this because this kind of specific activity wasn't recorded. Now, you look incredulous. I looked incredulous."

"Has the American taxpayer been getting his money's worth from such films?" Wallace asked.

"Oh, I don't think so," Weinberger replied. "I don't think all of them are necessary by any manner and means. Some are; some perform a useful function. But, by and large, there is too much being done and it's the kind of thing that feeds on itself because one department does it, another department feels it has to, and more and more people get involved. There's a competitive thing involved and it just gets completely out of hand, as it has been."

Remarked Wallace, "One gets the feeling that there are a bunch of junior Cecil B. De Milles here in Hollywood on the Potomac, making films for sometimes who knows what reason."

Added Goldwater, in his inquiry into these activities, "I would say that the . . . taxpayers are supporting productions they don't really need."

Weinberger, meanwhile, did call for "a much closer look in each department, from the top down, as to the volume of it, first of all; and secondly, as to the necessity; and thirdly, as to what real lasting value is it to the American public."

One conclusion is clear: With the exception of legitimate propaganda, intelligence, and defense-related needs, there is absolutely no need for the government to be in the film-making business. The average taxpayer might well ask why his hard-earned tax dollars should be spent teaching manners to officers or for a dozen films on how to brush one's teeth.

The government—with the few exceptions noted—should sell its movie equipment, phase out its audiovisual employees and "actors," and get out of the film business lock, stock, and barrel. If the government's entire film-producing efforts suddenly ended tomorrow, no one would notice. Its existence is the classic example of unending government extravagance and outrageous duplication. It must stop.

3

Selective Service

4

National Selective
Service Appeal Board

$45 Million

TODAY, UNDER THE LAW, NOT A SINGLE
American man is being drafted or can be drafted.

Yet the Selective Service continues on its merry way—apparently
oblivious to the all-volunteer army—and, when I last looked, had been
given a $45-million appropriation for the 1975 fiscal year to run its
nondrafting affairs.

America stopped the draft but the bureaucracy—thousands of state,
county, and local boards and appeal boards—goes on.

Section 10 (b) of the 1971 amendments to the Military Selective Service Act requires that the Selective Service System, despite expiration of
induction authority, maintain readiness in case of emergency mobilization requirements by continuing to register and classify young men.

But continuation of such standby readiness under the present circumstances is ridiculous. Military statistics indicate that the average length

of initial terms in Army Combat Arms is up by 45 percent, and that reenlistment by second-term volunteers was up 70 percent in the 1974 fiscal year.

"The morale and intelligence of the volunteer soldier is high and there are strong indications that our military forces are now both combat-ready and of sufficient strength to meet our military manpower needs," a 1974 Senate Appropriations Committee report concluded. Thus, while approving a new appropriation, the committee directed the Selective Service to explore vigorously "alternative less costly methods of maintaining a standby draft system, with particular emphasis on the increased use of volunteer registration and processing personnel.

"In light of very encouraging reports from both the Secretary of the Army and the Secretary of Defense concerning the success of the Volunteer Army, the committee feels that an accelerated winding-down of the Selective Service System's operations is justified in fiscal year '75," its report said.

The Selective Service insists that it cannot be prepared to provide the men necessary to maintain the armed forces at authorized strength through voluntary means. However, over 45,000 uncompensated citizens, including the members of local boards and advisers to registrants, help provide a host of registration and classification services and there is no reason that they cannot continue their service on the local level on a voluntary basis.

It is hard to argue for a system that cost taxpayers $53.7 million in 1974 after Congress abolished the need for that system. The volunteer armed forces, according to Defense Department and army reports, is succeeding. The nation has the military capability, as far as armed combat personnel are concerned, to handle any presently-envisioned emergency requiring troops. Should a far more serious military need arise, the Selective Service System, it seems obvious, could be geared up again with little trouble. The system of random selection by lottery has proven quite workable. Meanwhile, the Selective Service and the National Selective Service Appeal Board should be summarily discharged from duty.

5

National Science Foundation Social Science Research Programs

$49.5 Million

FOR ALL THE WORTHWHILE RESEARCH AND study the National Science Foundation has funded, the fact remains that it has wasted millions of dollars on study projects that even to the most scientific-minded virtually defy understanding. Many of these research projects fall within the NSF's social science programs, an area of inquiry vague enough to allow almost worthless ideas and theories— or at best very low priority ones—to be researched at the expense of the taxpayer.

And if anyone has deluded himself into thinking that researchers, particularly social scientists, are self-sacrificing academicians concerned primarily with the search for truth—and not with the material things of this world—salaries under these NSF programs shatter that mythology. Chief researchers on projects in NSF's social science program are being paid at an annual rate of up to $45,000—more than the $42,500 earned by members of Congress.

Here are a few examples of the types of projects NSF spent $35.6 million on during the 1973 fiscal year and an additional $49.5 million in fiscal 1975:

● Facility for Research on Language Behavior in the Chimpanzee. This is a $135,000 project to build a compound for use in research aimed at finding out whether chimpanzees can be taught to talk (I thought Tarzan had answered that question years ago!), and at answering a more fundamental question, What is language?

● Trends in Tolerance of Nonconformity is a $350,000 project to develop data on the changing effects of sociological variables (such as age, urbanization, religion, education, and social class) on the attitude of tolerance.

● Newari Psycho-Social Processes is a $55,200 study of two communities in Nepal to examine the "goodness of fit" between psychological orientations of individuals and the sociocultural matrix.

● Public Expectations About War is a $34,500 study to explore the public opinion trends in response to questions, asked between 1944 and the early 1960s, such as, "Do you expect us to fight in another war within the next _____ years?"

● Cognitive Configurations of a City is an $83,100 project to study a fairly large American city (Columbus, Ohio) to show how coherent cognitive structures emerge over time as information about the city develops.

● Public Ritual and Power is a $43,300 study of the nature of legitimacy in a colonial society focusing on the development of social and political theory and its relationship to large-scale public ceremonies developed by the British in 19th-century India.

● Adaptation and Minority Status is a $66,000 study of the social attitudes and modes of adaptation of the Korean minority in Japan in comparison with those characterizing the Japanese majority group on the one hand and, on the other, the former pariah caste of Burakumin.

Other research grants include: Early Phases of Hominid and Pongid Evolution, $55,500; Prehistory of Taiwan, $65,200; Prehistoric Urban-Rural Relationships, $28,600; Organizations, Decisions and Welfare, $32,700; Calculus of Social Networks, $105,000; Investigations of Ancient Mathematical Astronomy, $36,300; Early History of the Measurement of Motion, $14,700; Influence of Dyadic Relationships on

Adherence to Stressful Decisions, $46,600; and Unintentional Influence in Dyadic Interaction, $50,300.

The principal researcher in charge of a project titled Interpersonal Relations Within the Family was paid $7,212 for two months' work, an average of about $43,000 annually. Another researcher involved in a study called Conflict, Justice and Cooperation was paid $7,575 for two months' summer work, or an average of about $45,000 a year.

There is a need for research to cure the afflicted and to make the world a cleaner, safer, and healthier place to live. But certainly every area of inquiry financed by the taxpayer must first meet at least two fundamental tests: Is such research of top-priority importance to human welfare? And, can it be financed through the private sector? Perhaps, in some areas of scientific endeavor, these are tough questions to answer. But these and similar NSF research projects clearly do not meet the test of need and should be ended.

6

Small Business Administration

$444 Million

EVEN THOSE WHO FAVOR SOME PROGRAM TO aid America's small businesses must concede that the Small Business Administration's record is one of the government's grossest examples of bureaucratic corruption and political favoritism.

A cursory reading of the evidence presented to the House Banking and Currency Committee's Small Business Subcommittee by its investigators would be enough to shock even the most skeptical into agreeing that SBA should be brought to an end until its vast loan programs can be subjected to the most thorough scrutiny. Yet despite revelations of cronyism and political favoritism in the granting of millions of dollars in SBA loans—as well as ongoing Justice Department investigations and prosecutions—Congress went ahead in 1974 and approved legislation that raised SBA's overall lending ceiling from $6 billion to $7.3 billion and continued its authority through the 1975 fiscal year. Total SBA appropriations for salaries, operations, and business and disaster loans for fiscal 1975 was $444 million.

House Banking Committee chairman Wright Patman said in a report accompanying the SBA bill that congressional hearings had "revealed the existence of self-dealing, favored treatment and shaky if not fraudulent loan practices existing in a number of SBA offices around the country.

"My misgivings over the present and future condition of the Small Business Administration program have given rise to the question of whether the Small Business Administration itself should be abolished," Patman said. "Certainly its continued existence without extensive reform cannot be condoned."

The former House chairman said the evidence uncovered by the subcommittee's investigators "makes it painfully clear that loan guarantees provide an easy path for corrupt Agency officials and irresponsible bankers to waste the resources of the SBA program on unqualified borrowers at the expense of the taxpayers."

Another Democratic committee member, Frank Annunzio of Illinois, said he voted to report the legislation out of committee "not because of the SBA but in spite of it." Incredibly, after widely publicized hearings exposing SBA fraud and corruption, Congressman Annunzio said his vote was "in no way . . . intended to be an endorsement of the operations of the Small Business Administration." And in the same breath he charged, "It is my belief that the SBA is more interested in covering up than in cleaning up its operations. I detect a 'Watergate mentality' within the higher echelon of the SBA."

Only Wisconsin's Senator William Proxmire could not see continuing an agency so rife with mismanagement and called for abolishing it. Proxmire, a Democrat, said that despite SBA's enormous budget, only "a small proportion of businesses are helped, far less than one percent of eligible businesses. . . ." The Wisconsin fiscal watchdog soundly concluded, "The expense and bureaucracy don't merit the cost."

Like most federal loan programs, its true cost to the taxpayer is difficult to measure. SBA's operational budget for fiscal 1975 was only a tiny fraction of the over $5 billion it had outstanding as of 1974 in total loans, loan guarantees, and other obligations, excluding emergency disaster loans.

Created by Congress in 1953, SBA has seemingly countless loan programs, but only in recent years have they grown by billions of dollars. Its fundamental purpose is to aid and assist the interests of small businesses. Congress has expanded that simple goal with vast loan and loan-guarantee programs to help minority-owned businesses, small government contractors, small business investment companies, and other small entrepreneurs, including disaster assistance loans. There are three basic types of loans made by SBA: subsidized bank loans, which are guaranteed by SBA and for which the banks can charge up to 10.5 percent; matching loans, in which both the bank and SBA divide the loan; and direct low-interest loans, in which SBA provides funds at long-term rates as low as 5.5 percent.

Yet in recent years, according to the House subcommittee's hearing records,* SBA regional offices have approved loans and loan guarantees on the basis of favoritism and sometimes White House pressure. Much of the money has gone not to small businessmen but to the rich.

One example involved a former football player who served as co-chairman of Athletes for Nixon in 1968 and 1972. He obtained SBA approval for guaranteed bank loans totaling $250,000 for his Portsmouth, Va., construction firm, despite the fact that he had frequently written bad company checks and had defaulted on building contracts. After refusal by the bank to make the loans, despite the guarantees, the contractor was given a guaranteed line of credit by SBA in 1973 in the amount of $110,000 with another bank. Defaulting on his payments, the contractor was refused by the banker any additional loan money because, in the latter's words, it would be "pouring money down a rathole."

According to subcommittee investigators, the contractor as of the end of 1973 tried to obtain a direct SBA loan of $100,000 but was turned down by the regional office despite pressure to approve the loan from the central Washington office. A memo in the contractor's SBA files from the SBA district director to another SBA official involved in processing the loan papers stated: "Cassie, Please get out papers on McRae [the contractor] as quickly as possible. This is a White House case and the heat is on."

Another example cited by investigators involved an automotive equip-

---

* *Oversight Investigation of the Small Business Administration.* Hearings before the Subcommittee on Small Business of the House Banking and Currency Committee, Nov. 27, 28, 29, 30, and Dec. 4, 10, 11, 1973.

ment firm in Springfield, Va., whose principal officeholder was the father-in-law of the district director's personal secretary. He obtained a $30,000 direct loan at about half (5.5 percent) the going market interest rate with no minority enterprise connection whatsoever. Under agency regulations, loans involving SBA employees require prior approval by an ad hoc committee in Washington. However, the loan was not sent to the committee until after it was approved by officials. Moreover, one of the conditions of such loans is that the SBA employee involved must have nothing to do with processing the loan. Yet the secretary in question wrote a memo asking an SBA employee to "go ahead and order the check" for her father-in-law's firm. In addition, the proceeds from the loan were used personally to pay the loan recipient $3,400 based on a $7 per hour rate for labor in repairs he himself made to his own building. Not only that, but he apparently advanced a large amount of money to renovate his building out of his own pocket and then reimbursed himself from the SBA loan, indicating he had enough funds to handle the project without an SBA loan.

But SBA not only makes loans to small business enterprises. It approved a disaster loan of $4 million at one percent interest over 20 years to the Virginia Electric Power Company. This despite a statement in the loan file from the Washington central office stating that an earlier proposed 10-year maturity term was "excessive for a business which is able to repay the stockholders more than 10 times the amount of the loan in annual dividends."

Still another example of SBA hanky-panky involved the Petroleum Engineering Company of Norfolk, Va., which sought a $300,000 loan guarantee but was turned down by two SBA loan officers. Despite an attempt by higher officers to get the loan approved, it was turned down again by the same two men. On the day it was finally disapproved for the second time, a revised application was submitted for only $150,000. However, this time the application was not routed to the two loan officers who had rejected it in the first instance but instead went to two other SBA officials, who approved the loan.

Probably one of the most shocking examples of SBA loan-making abuse uncovered by subcommittee investigators involved Joseph Palumbo, a Charlottesville, Va., insurance executive and real estate developer. He is also the major stockholder in a Virgin Islands bank and has a net worth of more than $1 million.

The subcommittee, during its hearings, was presented with an elaborate chart by investigators showing how Palumbo and a number of companies in which he had holdings and served as an officer applied for a total of more than $11.6 million in loans, lease guarantees, loan guarantees, and contract awards. Not all of these loans were given final approval, it must be noted, and not all of the approved loans were disbursed. Of far more importance, however, is the fact that all of the loan-guarantee applications were approved by the SBA's Richmond office, although they were subsequently either turned down by higher authorities or canceled after the subcommittee investigators uncovered them. Underlying the entire case was the key fact that Palumbo was the brother-in-law of the SBA office's district director.

The hearing's record is spread out over 599 pages and describes in lurid detail even more shocking examples of SBA loan-making activities. Curtis A. Prins, the Banking Committee's chief investigator, testified that these and other instances were "no isolated cases. I think we have in our files a large number of cases that involve similar type loans." Prins' investigation also discovered that SBA files had been "tampered" with to conceal evidence and that it was "not unusual to find documents missing" from the agency's files. "In fact, we uncovered several loans that were made where there was not even a loan application in the file. The paperwork is extremely sloppily done, missing and in fact . . . some of the processing down there borders on dereliction of duty," he said.

Prins centered his investigation on the SBA's regional office in Richmond, Va., but said other SBA offices deserved further scrutiny, including Milwaukee, Dallas, Casper (Wyo.), Denver, Los Angeles, Albuquerque, Atlanta, Philadelphia, New York, Chicago, Washington, Kansas City, New Orleans, Birmingham, San Francisco, Boston, Baltimore, Miami, San Diego, Wilkes-Barre, and Cleveland.

Little more needs to be said about the SBA. Both its defenders and its critics tell the story. What remains almost impossible to understand is why Congress—after hearing these and dozens of other "horror" stories about its activities—decided to extend its authority. The whole process of subsidized loans withdraws needed capital from the private lending market and makes it that much more difficult for the great mass of small businesses to obtain necessary loans. Meantime, there is evidence that the SBA has been turning over millions of dollars, not to small businesses, but to big capital investors. And the taxpayer is picking up the tab. As with the Export-Import Bank and other government loan programs, it is difficult to determine just how much taxpayers are paying out in subsidies for low-interest loans and delinquent loan guarantees.

Meanwhile, there are strong indications that the "horrors" of Richmond may lurk in dozens of other SBA offices. Clearly, the agency does little—for all its billions—for the millions of truly deserving small business people in America, although it does a great deal for their taxes.

7

Civil Defense
Preparedness Agency

$82 Million

OVER THE PAST 10 YEARS THE GOVERNMENT
has spent over $1 billion for civil defense in the United States. Yet one
wonders whether all that money has made America any better protected
in the event of a nuclear attack.

In the early 1960s bomb shelters became popular, particularly when
the Cuban missile crisis heated world tensions. There was one proposal
before Congress to appropriate half a billion dollars to implement a na-
tionwide shelter program. The idea, even in the midst of that tense atmosphere, was shelved by Congress.

The bulk of the agency's funds are parceled out through a system of
50 percent matching grants to the states and communities to support
some 6,200 full-time and part-time civil defense personnel, and to
provide a national shelter system, warning sound devices, and civil
defense training. An additional 700 federal employees based in Wash-

ington and in eight regional offices around the country are also provided for under its budget. In the 10 years prior to 1974 Congress provided this agency with over $959.2 million to conduct its civil defense programs. Meanwhile, the Defense Department also spent billions of dollars on a vast and complex range of early warning and detection systems and various strategic defense capabilities.

Of 20,000 localities in the United States only about 5,000 are involved in the federal civil defense program. In many communities the so-called 24-hour watch of civil defense is the local police department, fire station, or sheriff's office. With the exception of the local civil defense directors on the state and local level, the bulk of the paid employees are part time; civil defense has become a way of earning extra money. "The shelter programs, the evacuation programs, the contribution and donation programs are sterling examples of make-work," says Sen. William Proxmire.

Some agency functions, such as warning of impending natural disasters, are obviously important, and they should be transferred to existing agencies concerned with emergencies such as the National Weather Service and the National Red Cross.

At one time, perhaps, when the nuclear might of the two major powers had to be delivered in planes and dropped over their targets, there was a case for such a civil defense effort. But in this nuclear age of long-range missiles, carrying multiple independently targeted reentry vehicles (MIRVS), there is virtually no place to hide from attack. The best protection today against a nuclear attack is a strong defense. Perhaps the $1 billion spent for this agency over the last 10 years could have been employed more usefully in building our national defenses.

8

Interstate Commerce Commission

$43.1 Million

SENATOR   PROXMIRE   BELIEVES   THAT
"there are more whiskers and cobwebs at the ICC than any place in the government.

"With fierce competition among air, rail, barge and road transportation, regulation for other than safety purposes has long been unnecessary," Proxmire says. *"The answer is abolition plus strong enforcement of the antitrust laws."*

It is accurate to say that many of the problems that now plague America's railroads, in fact the entire transportation industry, have been brought about by the smothering embrace of government regulation. An antiquated rate structure imposed on the railroads, in which rates are roughly figured on a ratio of value of the service to the shipper to the weight of the commodities shipped, has sown the seeds of destruction for rail carriers.

In his brilliant analysis of the cost of the ICC to the American economy, George W. Hilton stated: "Such a rate structure cannot survive in the face of competition, since the cost of the rival mode—mainly private trucking—becomes the principal alternative open to the shipper, and thus the actual measure of the value of rail service to him.

"The effort to preserve the traditional rate structure inevitably results in the loss of some rail traffic to trucking, thereby preventing as full utilization of rail plants as otherwise could occur."*

Congress, in a series of acts between 1887 and 1914, attempted to stop the rate wars between the giant railroads and proceeded to set railroad tariffs in which rates were figured on the value of the service rather than on what that service cost to provide. Thus, the decline of railroads began as industries sought out competitive alternatives to the railroad, and truck and barge transportation moved to fill their needs. Unfortunately, Congress wasn't content to stop there. It broadened the ICC in 1935 to include regulation of trucks and buses, and in 1940, water carriers. Thus, the ICC has become the overlord, as Hilton has correctly observed, of a noncompetitive industry, producing higher prices, and resulting in wasted resources and lower output, all at an increased cost to the economy and the public at large.

In effect, Hilton wrote, the ICC has bred a transportation cartel that, like a monopoly, "generates idleness. In railroading, idleness stems from the nature of the rate regulation, restrictions on exit from unprofitable activities, barriers to diversification, and the bias of regulation to present rail technology."

For example, the common carrier obligations of railroads often require them to carry shipments such as livestock, a task better handled by other carriers. Meanwhile, empty cattle pens are seen throughout the railroad network. Moreover, the ICC has prevented the rails from mercifully amputating miles of underutilized tracks on branch lines that should long ago have been abandoned because they were no longer economically feasible to continue.

The railroad is not the only transportation industry that has been hurt by the ICC's overregulation. Truckers, too, as a result of regulatory re-

---

* "What Has the ICC Cost You and Me?" *Trains Magazine*, October 1972. Hilton is a prominent UCLA professor who has for years studied the transportation industry and is regarded as one of the country's foremost experts in this field.

strictions, suffer from underutilized facilities. Under the present regulatory system, both railroads and intercity trucking are comparable to a manufacturer operating at 50 percent of capacity. Trucks, for example, are required to make uneconomical semifilled hauls, empty backhauls, often on roundabout routes that could be shortened. Barge operators also are forced to make similar empty backhauls under a veritable tangle of ICC rulemaking. (It should be noted here that railroads are 100 percent regulated in their rates whereas trucking and barge rates for various commodities carried are only partially regulated. The "gypsy" truckers are not touched at all by ICC regulation.)

Some economists have argued persuasively that the ICC's present rate structure for railroads has resulted in a progressively larger volume of freight being diverted to trucks that could be more cheaply transported by rail. What is clear is that existing ground transportation regulation perpetuates the idleness of our transport resources, prohibits the most productive and economical mode of transportation from responding to the incentives of the marketplace, and results in higher costs to industry and, ultimately, the consumer. How much? Experts have estimated that the ICC's cartelization of the transportation industry costs society from $5 billion to $10 billion a year in higher consumer prices—or up to $200 a year for each average American family.

When all is said and done, what the ICC's ironclad rulemaking has produced for America is sheer waste. It has cemented the ground transportation industry into place with its rigid regulation and left no room for innovation, organizational overhaul, and movement of capital into more economical (and profitable) transportation.

Who profits from the present system? As Hilton pointed out: ". . . the avidity with which the American Trucking Association fights to preserve the present organization of the industry is the best possible indication that the major truckers benefit from the cartelization. In a competitive framework, they would be beset by rate-cutting railroads . . . and by a vast inflow of independent truckers, mainly from minority groups, offering basic, cheap service."

Congress obviously wanted to avoid the ICC's slow and cumbersome machinery when it created both Amtrak (the government-operated rail passenger service) and the U.S. Railroad Administration—the government's attempt to save the railroad's freight service in the Northeast—because it virtually bypassed the ICC in the latter's day-today operations. Amtrak can raise or lower its fares and change its routes at will without going to the ICC for approval. The same is generally true for the USRA, where the ICC is given largely an advisory role in its affairs. If the ICC were to disappear tomorrow, it would have not the slightest effect on either Amtrak or USRA. Congress did give the ICC power to set certain standards governing Amtrak's services but by the time the ICC lumbered forth with its recommendations, Amtrak was already in the process of adopting standards of its own.

Perhaps at one time a persuasive case was made for the government's operating the ICC, but that case can no longer be made effectively. Its demise would go a long way toward allowing America's transportation industries to offer cheaper, more efficient, and more productive service.

9

Civil Aeronautics Board

$84.8 Million

THERE IS NOTHING SACROSANCT ABOUT THE Civil Aeronautics Board (CAB). Just because it has been around for nearly 40 years, doesn't mean it should be around for another 40. One need only look at the condition of U.S. airlines today to determine that federal regulation has cramped, not expanded, the airline industry. We can do without the CAB.

The CAB is in charge of promoting and regulating civil air transportation within the United States and between the U.S. and foreign countries. Its primary duties include setting rates and fares U.S. and foreign air carriers may charge, and granting subsidies to domestic airlines that provide air service to areas where passenger demand is insufficient to support such service.

Many of the arguments against the Interstate Commerce Commission can similarly be used against the CAB. By setting anticompetitive rates for all carriers, the CAB prohibits free competition between airlines and thus forces the airlines into other forms of needless competition, such as overcompetition on minor routes, and too frequent scheduling of flights. The result is that the airlines are too often empty and needed capital is being wasted. The CAB prevents the airlines from offering the lowest possible fares and instead drives them into competing over the number of daily flights one airline may offer over another into a particular city, the number of meal choices and movies it offers on a flight, and other costly gimmicks. Thus, the consumer is denied the fruit of true price competition: efficient service at the lowest possible price. Air passengers are given no substantive choice and are forced to pay the fares set by the CAB.

By removing restrictions on fares, the airlines could legitimately compete for the nation's airfare business on routes where the demand for travel will support a profit. (Unfortunately, the CAB has for years prevented the airlines from getting together even to talk about mutual reduction of services.) The antitrust laws would of course govern any airline mergers and proposed acquisitions.

The CAB's track record on promoting air transportation in America can be seen best in one simple statistic: In 1938, when the agency began, there were 19 major trunk lines in the United States. As of 1974, there were 11. Author-editor M. Stanton Evans found it "somewhat astonishing to reflect that, over the entire history of the CAB, there has not been a single new trunk line founded—in an industry field that has been marked by rapid technological advance and explosive growth."

But the CAB has prohibited competition not only in airfares but in other areas as well, banning fare discounts for youth, tourist excursions, and even preventing certain European carriers from offering cuts in transatlantic rates.

One of the clearest comparative examples of how the CAB's rate structure affects the domestic market can be found in the state of California, which is large enough to support intrastate airlines that are not subject to CAB regulations. A competitive market thrives in California with such carriers as Pacific Southwest Airways charging rates that are half those of the CAB trunks. Leonard Ross of Columbia University Law School determined that a ticket from Los Angeles to San Francisco cost about 4.8 cents a mile, while it cost 9.9 cents a mile to fly from Boston to Washington, D.C. Studies by Dr. Theodore Keeler of the

University of California at Berkeley indicate that federal regulation, on the average, has resulted in a fare increase of about 74 percent on passengers flying interstate lines compared to intrastate carriers.

The CAB's anticompetitive and inflationary impact has been strongly criticized by none other than Lewis A. Engman, chairman of the Federal Trade Commission. Engman estimated that total government regulation of the transportation industry may cost consumers up to $16 billion a year.

The FTC chief called CAB's regulatory practices "government-sanctioned price fixing" and noted that because of the agency's ironclad control of the airline industry, new competitive airlines had been frozen out of the industry. In late 1974, for example, the CAB rejected an application by Laker Airways, a privately owned British airline, which proposed to fly regularly scheduled flights from New York to London, offering low, $125 one-way fares—about one-third the "economy" rate charged at that time by TWA and Pan American.

In a hard-hitting speech delivered in Detroit, October 7, 1974, Engman recited the case of Pacific Southwest Airways, observing that the major regulated airlines were forced into trying "to make a fat profit on a high-volume run like Los Angeles-to-San Francisco because it knows it is going to lose a bundle flying between Black Rock and Where Am I City, which the CAB, with the full support of concerned and interested members of Congress, requires it to do." He totally rejected this type of "book balancing act," which, he said, the CAB forced on airlines so as to require customers to pay higher fares on other flights in order to support a network of lesser traveled routes that "no longer and perhaps never did" meet the cost-profit test of consumer demand. Thus, Engman added, airline competition has been reduced by the CAB to a single unregulated area, consumer service. "That is why the average airline commercial looks like an ad for a combination bawdy house and dinner theater."

Of the CAB's $84.8-million budget for fiscal 1975, $17.1 million was for salaries and other operational expenses, while $67.7 million went for subsidy payments to various air carriers. The rationale for the taxpayer subsidizing airlines is that it helps provide air transportation to small communities that would otherwise be without such services. But the subsidy also indirectly places the government in direct competition with other transportation carriers in these areas, namely buses and trains (not to mention small airline firms that can't compete with government-subsidized airlines). Obviously, if air travel proves unprofitable in a particular area or region, then a rail or bus line in those areas would absorb whatever transportation demands existed, particularly to and from the nearest point where air travel was provided.

Perhaps the most convincing and authoritative argument against the CAB's subsidies has been made by George Eads, author of the *Local Service Airline Experiment,* published by the Brookings Institution. Eads says, "The case for a complete end to the 'local service experiment' appears to be a strong one. No convincing evidence has been discovered that any substantial benefits accrue to the nation at large from the continued expenditure of federal funds to support local air service. Furthermore, the fact that total passenger originations either remained constant or declined between 1968 and 1969 at 67 percent of the points serviced exclusively by the local service carriers indicates that even the prime beneficiaries of the subsidy—the travelers who fly for considerably less than cost—believe that the value of the service provided is declining. Traffic was static or declined at 71 percent of the exclusively served cities of less than 25,000 population. Even prior to the establishment of the local service carriers and the postwar expansion of the trunk lines, air service was within easy reach of a substantial proportion of the population. As early as 1938, the average population of cities that were not served was only 11,595, and the average distance from the nearest city with air service was only 35 miles. When account is taken of the probable entry of unsubsidized air taxis at many points if the local service carriers suspended service to them, it is quite conceivable that 97 percent of the metropolitan population, that proportion that the local service carriers claimed to be serving in 1969, would still have easy access to scheduled air service even if the local service subsidy were ended."

The arguments against government subsidies for the airlines received little real attention until Pan American World Airways asked the CAB for a $10.2-million-a-month bailout to stay in business. Pan Am argued that it was in the "national interest" to keep the U.S. airline alive;

---

* "The Impact of Regulations on the Local Service Airline Subsidy," by George Eads, which was drawn from his book, was published by the Joint Economic Committee of Congress in a report entitled "The Economics of Federal Subsidy Programs," Part 6—Transportation Subsidies.

that it was a mark of prestige for Americans to maintain its flagship service abroad among more than 20 other foreign airlines, which are substantially or entirely owned by their governments.

Columnist George F. Will said it perfectly when he wrote that "Americans, as taxpayers and as travelers, can get along without Pan Am. If foreign governments think they get prestige from operating airlines at a loss, that is bad for Pan Am but it is nice for the rest of us. If foreign governments want to fly people across the Atlantic for less than it costs to do so, let's let them provide all the transatlantic traffic. If American travelers—a generally affluent lot—are going to benefit from government subsidies, let the subsidies come from foreign governments."

The arguments against subsidies to Pan Am apply equally to the CAB's existing subsidy program.

As for other CAB responsibilities, it is also authorized to approve all air route applications and assign them in conformity with necessary travel and safety requirements. This obviously essential chore, along with other needed CAB regulatory responsibilities, could easily be divided up between the Federal Aviation Administration and the National Transportation Safety Board.

10

Women's Bureau

$1.9 Million

WHEN THE WOMEN'S BUREAU WAS CREATED BY Congress in 1920 there was no doubt that women needed all the help they could get to obtain better jobs and better pay in every sector of American life. But with the advances made today by women (sometimes despite women's liberation) for equal pay for equal work, this agency has become a bureaucratic anachronism that is no longer needed.

According to the *U.S. Government Organization Manual,* the Women's Bureau is located within the Labor Department's Employment Standards Administration and is responsible for "formulating standards and policies which shall promote the welfare of wage earning women, improve their working conditions, increase their efficiency, advance their opportunities for professional employment, and investigate and report on all matters pertinent to the welfare of women in industry."

But in reality this bureau has become a legislative lobbying outfit that uses the taxpayers' money to mobilize support for such controversial measures as the Equal Rights Amendment, helps to provide women speakers for various organizations, and pours out expensive literature about careers for women and statistics on the female labor force.

Ostensibly, the bureau is concerned with job discrimination against women and ensuring federal contract compliance with federal sex discrimination laws. It also works toward broadening career and education opportunities for women both in government and in the private sector. Its Division of Economic Status Opportunities also publishes mountains of data dealing with the economic status of women. It is a waste because all of these areas are being handled by other major agencies within the Labor Department and far more thoroughly than the Women's Bureau could ever hope to do. And the bureau is the first to admit it: "We're really an information and referral service," a spokeswoman for the bureau told me. "We are constantly referring people to other agencies."

The bureau also spends much of its time helping to organize and promote conferences and meetings for women's groups and initiates and fights for legislation allegedly beneficial to women, such as the Equal Rights Amendment to the Constitution, about which there is strong disagreement throughout the country. The bureau began lobbying for the controversial amendment in 1970, according to one spokeswoman.

The Women's Bureau also operates 10 regional offices throughout the country but admits "they do pretty much what we do here" in Washington.

There are numerous bureaus and offices within the massive U.S. Department of Labor and all of them conduct programs that concern men *and* women. The U.S. Employment Service, the Employment Standards Administration, the Office of Federal Contract Compliance, the Occupational Safety and Health Administration, the Bureau of Labor Statistics, and the separate Equal Employment Opportunity Commission—all are agencies concerned with the labor force, and that includes women. By the bureau's own admission it either passes on complaints and inquiries by women to these and other agencies or else uses data and services supplied by these same agencies.

At one time, when admittedly not enough women were employed in government, the bureau may have been necessary. Today that is no longer the case. The agency is duplicating work already being handled by other Labor Department offices. Women should no longer be placed by government on a separate work reservation all their own. They are part, and a growing part, of the total labor force and their problems should be the concern of the entire Labor Department, not to mention the entire nation.

11

National Highway Traffic Safety Administration

$170.9 Million

WITNESSING THE RISING HUMAN CARNAGE on our nation's highways over the years is the most conclusive evidence one needs to prove that this agency has failed to make highway traffic significantly safer.

Between 1967—when the agency began—and 1973, annual highway traffic deaths rose from 52,924 to 56,056. The National Highway Traffic Safety Administration began with an $11.3 million budget in 1967. By fiscal 1975 it had skyrocketed to $170.9 million. Even though the 1975 budget had grown more than 15 times, the death rate kept climbing.

Then, after hundreds of thousands of lives and hundreds of millions of dollars, the supreme irony occurred. In January 1974 Congress, by one simple act—which cost the taxpayers not a single cent—brought about a drastic decrease in highway fatalities. It simply ordered, amidst the energy crisis, a national speed limit of 55 miles per hour, not to save lives but to conserve energy. The National Safety Council says that highway deaths dropped by 9,600 in 1974.*

All the millions of tax dollars spent by the government on automotive studies, research, and testing had failed to curb the spiraling death toll. In 1974 more Americans were getting to where they wanted to go by automobile without an accident because of this simple and sane act of Congress.

Declared NHTSA administrator James Gregory: "We've found continuously over the last few months since it's [the 55 mph limit] been in effect that we have gotten very close to consistent 20 percent reduction in fatalities on the highway." Gregory said there were other reasons for the reduced fatalities, including less driving because of the fuel shortage. But "the reduction in speed, or what happens when people go at a lower speed, is the big factor" in sharply reducing deaths, he noted. By September 1974 both houses of Congress had voted overwhelmingly to make the 55-mile-per-hour speed limit permanent. The Senate Public Works Committee, in its report on the limit, said it had "produced the single most effective improvement in highway safety in recent years." The committee cited a Gallup poll showing 72 percent of those Americans interviewed favored the lower limit.

All of this must be weighed against NHTSA's ongoing programs. For all the millions of dollars in research and development to try to make the automobile accident-proof seem to fly in the face of an immovable fact: drivers, not automobiles, cause accidents. And, by and large, safer drivers are not going to be produced in Washington. They are going to be developed by daring, innovative programs carried out within the 50 states and their communities. Safer cars can also help reduce fatalities and injuries but that is something the automotive industry can do, I think, without resorting to direct federal spending, which I'll discuss later in this chapter.

It is time for Congress to think through its present approach to highway safety and to ask itself these questions: Are we effectively and wisely spending hundreds of millions of tax dollars on this problem? Or are we throwing money away?

Congress has already provided stunning replies to two of NHTSA's

---

* According to National Safety Council statistics, 55,800 people died in 1973 in automobile accidents. In 1974, with the 55-mile-per-hour speed limit in force, there were 46,200 such deaths.

flagship projects: the mandatory seat belt-ignition interlock system and the mandatory installation of the air bag, or passive restraint device. The response to each: an overwhelming no!

Taken together, the two proposals represent Big Brotherism in all its wicked tyranny. The interlock-belts had become mandatory with the 1974 car models. The air bags, under NHTSA's plans, are to be required for the 1977 models. However, the House in August 1974 voted 339-49 to bar the Transportation Department from making either the interlock-belt system or the air bag mandatory. It approved a bill that instead would have made either of them optional, starting with the 1977 models. The Senate also overwhelmingly voted against the interlock-belt. Compromise legislation worked out in a Senate-House conference in early October 1974 totally banned the interlock system. However, the measure gave the Secretary of Transportation authority to order installation of the air bag, unless vetoed by Congress within 60 days. (Considering the intensity of opposition to the interlock, Congress may very well ban the bags, too.)

The seat belt-ignition system prohibits a motorist from starting his car until the seat belt has been fastened. It is expensive, subject to malfunction, and disliked by almost everyone. Columnist James J. Kilpatrick said it had been invented "by the same devilish genius that in times past contrived thumbscrews, the iron maiden and the rack. Why has a benevolent government saddled this imposition upon the people? It is because a benevolent government believes it knows what is best for the people. . . . Big Brother is watching over us." The House even voted to bar a requirement that buzzers go off when the belts are not buckled—such was the intensity of opposition to the government forcing people to use them.

The air bag device, which balloons out of the steering wheel upon impact, would also have proven costly if required in every car, adding an estimated $250 onto new car prices. The NHTSA said the bags would save thousands of lives each year. But the American Automobile Association (AAA) said the air bags would cost consumers 100 percent more than they would return in safety benefits. In fact, the AAA study* showed that either alone or used with safety belts, the benefits of the

---

* Directed by Dr. Lawrence A. Goldmuntz, former assistant director for civil technology in the White House Office of Science and Technology and onetime executive director of the Federal Council of Science and Technology.

bags could never justify the additional cost to motorists: an estimated $3.65 billion annually.

The AAA also maintained there was "no evidence"—NHTSA to the contrary notwithstanding—to show that air bags approach "the known lifesaving capabilities of properly worn belt-harness systems." It also found the air bag to be effective primarily in frontal crashes, while only marginally effective in side impacts, rollovers, or rear-end and multiple crashes. The AAA report also emphasized that no individual using an American harness was known to have been killed in a crash, other than a collision where the passenger compartment of the vehicle itself was crushed or invaded by some outside object. "In these cases no restraint system would have spared the occupant," said the AAA.

James L. Buckley, Conservative-Republican senator from New York, who had introduced legislation to do much of what the House ban attempted, said prohibition of mandatory seat belt systems and air bag installation would "remove the grasping hand of Big Brother government from the lives of American citizens." A number of Senate liberals cosponsored the proposed ban, including Missouri's Thomas Eagleton, who declared: "If freedom is to have any meaning in this country, it certainly must encompass the right of an individual to lead his life as he sees fit, so long as it does not interfere directly with the similar pursuit by others."

Of the agency's total fiscal 1975 budget of $170.9 million, $73.4 million went for a variety of vehicle-testing, research, and development projects, including the testing of parts, tires, and other equipment. Over $2 million was budgeted to study pedestrian and bicycle safety, among other things, and to run a mass-media safety campaign.

Most of the remaining $96 million went to the states in the form of grants to help finance driver licensing, motor vehicle registration, traffic records, police traffic services, driver education, automobile inspection, and a number of other services. According to NHTSA spokesmen, many of these grants are part of a federal effort to make various state-testing, inspection, and other motor vehicle laws uniform throughout the country. I may be getting my priorities mixed up, but it seems to me that reducing deaths and injuries should come first in any highway safety program. If that happens, then we might consider the need for nationally uniform traffic safety laws (at the moment the seriousness of its need escapes me).

NHTSA's programs, then, can be basically divided into two categories: research and development, and grants to the states. As far as its research programs are concerned, the rising death toll, before Congress acted, speaks for itself. Work on stronger, more resilient bumpers, improvements in windshield glass, the collapsible steering wheel, steel beam guards, and all the rest have not turned the death rate around—irrespective of the mathematical arguments that there are more deaths because there are more cars.

The improvements may be fine but it should be pointed out that all of them were developed by automobile manufacturers using federal money. There is no reason why this kind of research and development can't go on without additional direct federal spending. Simply provide the automotive industry with a tax incentive to invest more of its working capital into programs aimed at developing a safer automobile, one that can withstand a greater impact without injury to the occupants. Such an incentive might allow a percentage to be deducted from a corporation's taxable income if a certain share of its profit were reinvested into safety R & D programs.

As far as the grants are concerned, it seems to me that federal highway safety aid should be keyed to an incentive formula benefiting states actually reducing highway accidents. This approach is used to a limited extent in NHTSA's fiscal 1975 budget, which provides $16 million for incentive grants to states significantly reducing their highway fatality rate. Such a total incentive program of aid should probably be run by the Federal Highway Administration, which received $15 million under NHTSA's budget for its own highway-related safety grant program. Since the Federal Highway Administration is also given responsibility for improving state and local highway safety programs through matching grants, there is no reason why a portion of its mammoth $4.6-billion road building budget can't be used to give aid to state highway safety programs in lieu of NHTSA grants. What could be more relevant to building highways than the lives lost on them? Knowing they would have to crack down on highway speeders—the major cause of accidents—and develop effective programs to combat auto accidents, or else lose their funds, the states would no doubt be highly motivated to achieve their share of the funding. And to those who would object to using jealously guarded federal highway aid for highway safety programs, there is this answer: Sure, we need roads, but we border on gross negligence if we continue to pour all our highway money into road construction and ignore one consequence of roads—automobile accidents. Besides, with a permanent lower speed limit, rising fuel prices, and an ongoing fuel conservation effort, should we continue to move at top speed on our interstate highway building program? Meantime, under my proposal the states significantly curbing their death toll—and in the final analysis only the states can solve this stubborn problem—would be rewarded with bonus grants to help pay for more of their safety programs, which in turn would serve as models for other less successful states to emulate.

Of course, some NHTSA programs should be retained, particularly its Alcohol Safety Action Projects, which have brought about some reductions in alcohol-related fatalities. Aid to driver education programs in the schools also have their beneficial effects. These could be transferred to HEW. Other programs that provide funding for highway maintenance programs, such as breakaway signs and poles and crash-easing sand-filled barrels cushioning road abutments, could also be handled by the Federal Highway Administration.

Meanwhile, we would be able to save most of the spending that is now going for NHTSA's budget, not the least of which is $3.3 million for salaries and administrative expenses alone.

12

National Foundation on the Arts and Humanities

$159 Million

. . . I reached under her belly, to the squack, and what an idea escaped the boundary of my polemic gush brain! To frig and to publish! Hands trembling I slashed her with the pud, one hand cranking the mimeo, the other steadying the orgasm donut. And the paper was fed through, printing the second edition of 'The Toe-Queen Poems,' kuh-plak kuh-plak kuh-plak kuh-plak, faster and faster . . .

THIS EXCERPT, FROM A WORK ENTITLED "The Hairy Table," by Ed Saunders, had been chosen by a panel of judges to be included in an anthology of new fiction published under a grant from the National Endowment for the Arts to author and editor George Plimpton. Endowment chairwoman Nancy Hanks, fearing its appearance in the anthology would create a storm of controversy that could cost her agency millions in congressional appropriations, asked Plimpton to remove the piece from the literary collection or else face cancellation of the project's next volume. Plimpton, who had not read the story himself before it was included, at first resisted the obvious attempt at censorship and then caved in to Miss Hanks' demands. "The Hairy Table" did not appear in the anthology. It became a victim—and a classic example—of the heavy hand of government censorship in the arts.

But other dubious works did appear in the series of collections funded by the agency, which since 1965 has been distributing millions of dollars in grants to help support the arts, including orchestras, opera houses, museums, theaters, and other groups and individuals.

One now celebrated poem, the entire text of which consists of seven letters—"lighght"—received an award of $750, or about $107 per letter. Queried an aghast Rep. William Scherle (R.-Iowa), "Can anyone even pronounce this poem?"

Other works within the anthology contained four-letter words, vitriolic attacks against the U.S. military, and weird titles like "A-15" and "A-18." For example, Charles Zerner of Eugene, Oregon, was given $7,857 to study how "children at play utilize the urban environment as a theatrical and mythical arena." And the Moravian Music Foundation was given $79,675 to catalog its collection of manuscripts and music. Aldo Bernardo and Bernard Huppe, of the State University of New York at Binghamton, were given $31,912 to microfilm the principal archives of the island of Malta. And a humanities grant of $8,470 was awarded to study 19th-century political cartoons.

Sometimes the agency finances criticism of U.S. policies. In a 1967 essay in *Partisan Review*, Frederick C. Crews called American involvement in Vietnam "patent lunacy" and urged a study of "the Hitler within ourselves." During that same year, *Partisan Review* also published a poem by Frederick Seidel of Rutgers called "Freedom Bombs for Vietnam," which depicted the bombs as having "ears almost as large as the President's" (Lyndon Johnson's) and portrayed Dean Rusk as having a "smile that looks like incest." Mr. Seidel's work included this quaint imagery:

> A spit glob and naked flashbulbs pop in Rusk's ear
> And go down with whole heads, whole fields of heads
> Of Human hair, jagged necks attached.

Crews was awarded $1,000 for his artistic efforts (LBJ would have been livid) and Seidel received a $500 prize. The Endowment for the Arts also awarded *Partisan Review* $500 for publishing these and one other selection that year.

Other funded projects include the so-called experimental theaters. Over a five-year period the agency has given more than $1.5 million to these low-budget groups and supported experiments such as Robert Wilson's *The Life and Death of Joseph Stalin,* a "silent opera" that runs wordlessly and in slow motion for half a day, and Tom Eyen's *The Dirtiest Show on Earth,* described as a play of devil-may-care nudity that frolics to a sexual orgy for its dramatic climax. Republican congressman Robert W. Daniel, Jr. of Virginia cited a news report on Wilson's epic opera-in-silence which noted that it contained "a cast of over 100 adults, 18 children, a four-month-old baby, a number of gorillas, a goat, a dog, a sheep, and 32 dancing ostriches."

Said Daniel, "Now I would normally defend the right of Americans to engage in this sort of madness, except in this case . . . part of the tab . . . has been picked up by the long-suffering U.S. taxpayer."

In a *Washington Post* interview, Endowment deputy chairman Michael Straight told of a 1972 incident in which a dance company supported by Endowment grants performed at the Kennedy Center: "They did a dance which had a sound collage, and a man on the soundtrack announced that the United States had fought three wars in order to keep up the price of rice and oppress the blacks and extend the supremacy of the white man. . . ." Straight told an assistant to Sen. James L. Buckley, who had complained about taxpayers having to support such propaganda, that he was prohibited from interfering in any way with the dance company's program and that "we're doing a number of things in this category which would offend—for example, *The Trial of the Catonsville Nine,*" which was based on the transcript of the Berrigan trial. A *Washington Star* critic who reviewed the dance program found it "a little disturbing to think of how much [Black] Panther ideology may go into the schools with these cultural delights. . . ."

As to federal support for experimental theaters, Straight noted, "The government is actually playing a larger role in, say, assuring the continued existence of the experimental theaters than in assuring the existence of the Boston Symphony."

It is unarguable that the arts in America are intrinsic to the nation's cultural lifeblood. They always have been and they always will be, with or without a program of federal aid. This is a simple and fundamental premise to any discussion of federal aid to the arts. But if 12 men or women were picked at random to judge any form of art, one doubts they could ever reach an evaluative consensus on its merits. The arts are a profoundly subjective matter, determined in part by exposure, knowledge and personal sensitivities, whatever one is considering. Taxpayers who must pay for this program aren't in the enviable position of Sen. Claiborne Pell of Rhode Island, Democratic chairman of the special arts and humanities subcommittee, which oversees the agency. Pell can closely interrogate the Endowment directors to determine how much money is going for things like abstract paintings. "I don't like abstract art," Pell impresses upon the directors each year when their program comes under his review.

The arts, like most other things born of the private sector, must find their support among the people. If Americans will go to see a silent opera and support such an undertaking, fine. But if such art evokes little or no individual support, why should all the people be taxed to support it? The same holds true for museums, symphony orchestras, theaters, and every component of the nation's artistic life.

Listening to the Endowment's directors one comes away with the impression that they truly believe all these millions of dollars will lead to a renaissance in American art and humanities; that eventually, given enough money, the masses and the arts will one day converge in a blinding flash of light and the Golden Age of Greece will be reborn. "I look forward to the day when the workingman comes home, opens a can of beer, turns on the television and watches the Metropolitan," Straight gushed. It may come as a surprise to Mr. Straight, but there are men in America, common men, too, with little formal education, who do come home from work, open a can of beer and put *Turandot* on their stereo. They found the arts long before the National Endowment began doling out its millions. (I've long nurtured the suspicion that the National Endowment people really believe they discovered art for America.)

The dramatic rise in the number of orchestras and art galleries and theaters and exhibits in recent years far surpasses the confined parameters of the Endowment's aid program. Had the fund never existed, this growth would have taken place anyway because it draws its source of support freely from people who, one way or another, are involved and give. Certainly, financial assistance for large art institutions and organizations must come from the state and local governments within whose communities they were born. But business and foundations continue to be the major source of funding for all the arts—giving close to $300 million in 1973.* And that figure was expected to go much higher by the end of 1974. Individuals and philanthropists give many hundreds of millions more to the arts each year.

It should be emphasized that without the National Endowment for the Arts the government would still be making an ambitious contribution to the arts and humanities via the government-supported ($60 million) Public Broadcasting System. Also, within the U.S. Office of Education at least three-quarters of a million dollars a year is set aside for grants and contracts to encourage and assist state and local educational agencies to conduct programs of the arts within elementary and secondary schools. And, too, the Smithsonian Institution operates more than half a dozen museums and at least half a dozen major art galleries. The National Gallery of Art in Washington has added a $70-million art gallery to its complex (financed entirely by private funds) and operates for the schools an art exhibit program that serves about 4,000 communities a year. The Smithsonian also operates a traveling exhibit program. In addition, there are the famed Kennedy Center and Ford Theater in Washington. All this, by any standard, should be enough.

---

* Business Committee for the Arts, New York, New York.

13

**Coastal Plains
Regional Commission**

14

**Four Corners
Regional Commission**

15

**New England
Regional Commission**

16

**Old West
Regional Commission**

17

Ozarks
Regional Commission

18

Pacific Northwest
Regional Commission

19

Upper Great Lakes
Regional Commission

$42 Million

WITH THE ESTABLISHMENT OF THE APPALACHIAN
Regional Commission in 1965 as part of President Johnson's War on
Poverty, pressure began to build in Congress for similar federal commissions in almost every other region in the land. The consensus seemed to
be, "If Appalachia gets one, then we want one, too." Thus, Congress in
1965 authorized the creation of virtual "wall to wall" regional commissions.

Between 1966 and 1972 seven of them were established, covering 29
states.* By any intelligent assessment they have accomplished little

---

* Usually referred to as the Title V Commissions, established under the Public
Works and Economic Development Act of 1965.

despite all their millions of dollars. They should be abandoned.

The commissions are really an extension of the idea behind the Economic Development Administration (discussed in the next chapter) to initiate and spur long-range economic development in areas of severe unemployment and low income, primarily through an assortment of business and public works grants and loans. As originally envisioned, the commissions were to combat economic depressions on a regional basis, working in concert with state and local officials to see that federal money was placed where it was most needed. It didn't work out that way. Studies made of the commissions show they have been largely ineffective, in many cases duplicating similar federal programs.

Despite several attempts by the Nixon administration to terminate them, Congress has stubbornly kept them going in the face of strong evidence the commissions have failed to achieve their stated goals.

A joint report* by the Commerce Department and the Office of Management and Budget—which Congress requested—concluded in February 1974 that the commissions "have had very limited influence on the allocation of resources in their regions to create jobs for the unemployed in areas of persistent and substantial unemployment. Although many of the commissions have developed broad plans for dealing with unemployment problems in their regions, they have had little success in directing resources to help implement those plans."

The report also said that while there may be unusual instances in which a depressed region requires a joint effort by two or more states, the experience with the commissions indicated that "many economic adjustment problems are not multi-state in nature, and for such problems a regional commission serves little purpose."

Congress has approved blustering authorizations for the commissions in the past—$150 million for each of the 1975 and 1976 fiscal years— but when it came to the actual appropriation of money it always fell far short of its promises: $42 million for fiscal 1975. Not only has Congress given the commissions a low fiscal priority but past administrations have consistently made budget requests far lower than the funding originally sought by the commissions or their parent agency, the Commerce Department, in most cases more than 50 percent lower.

It is almost impossible to thread through the tangle of technical assist-

*"Report to the Congress on the Proposal for an Economic Adjustment Program," February 1, 1974, OMB-Commerce.

74

ance and demonstration projects, planning assistance grants, and public works financing, among the hundreds of projects funded by the commissions, and determine how a commission's federal dollars are supposed to help an area's economy. One economic impact study program in Arizona, in which I tried to trace through a maze of bureaucratic dollar shuffling, revealed that the money went from the commission to the state and in turn to a research firm in Ohio. I found that research and consulting firms end up receiving a large portion of the federal dollar in these programs. It's difficult to figure out how the jobless and low-income families are helped by economic studies that few people will ever read. Moreover, dollar for dollar these marginal programs have virtually little impact when compared to the job-creating effects of major federal programs such as defense, space, atomic energy, and highway construction. Yet, between 1967 and 1972 the commissions cost federal taxpayers over $120 million.

A 1974 analysis of these and other federal regional programs by the Brookings Institution concluded that the seven regional commissions "in general . . . have been organizations of limited accomplishment. . . ."* The study found that there was significant divisiveness and conflict between the various federal cochairmen, who are based in Washington, and the executive directors, who are based in the region's headquarters.

"Because federal funding has been so low, state governments have not felt much impact from the commissions' activity," the Brookings study said. "A pair of Department of Commerce consultants, after nearly a hundred interviews with state officials and others, concluded in 1970 that state officials perceived the commissions as 'interesting mechanisms in intergovernmental relations' which 'probably take more time than they are worth now in financial returns from the Federal Treasury.' "

Because regional commission proposals often are not checked out with each state's governor's office, governors, in New England at least, have often been surprised by projects being planned for their area. The Brookings study also noted complaints from state officials who said the commissions "sometimes imposed projects on the state."

The study also reached these conclusions about the seven commissions: "As a superstructure upon the more traditional structure of federal-state organization, they are a complicating feature, attractive to

* Martha Derthick, *Between State and Nation,* Brookings Institution, Washington, D. C.

the states for whatever money and services they yield, but not for their own sake." There may be specific areas of the country in which dire poverty and endemic unemployment—complicated by other severe economic conditions—require a regional approach, but "it should not be extended to the whole country," the study said. Such a coast-to-coast application of the regional concept has in effect placed "the needy region on a par with others, while giving extraordinary help to places whose need for it has not been demonstrated."

In stark contrast to the $42 million Congress gave to these commissions in 1975, lawmakers the same year also approved a $4.5-billion public works spending bill. Without getting into the whole question of this annual pork-barrel program, much of which could be trimmed, one would think that if Congress were really serious about boosting economically depressed regions, it would restructure its massive public works program and concentrate its billions on those severely stricken areas most in need of jobs and economic recovery. Instead, the billions are spread like confetti all over the country, irrespective of whether a region or state is economically prosperous or nearly indigent, each member of Congress insisting on his share of pork.

In the meantime, the studies done on these commissions show they are not working and should be terminated.

20

Economic Development Administration

$258.5 Million

IN 1974 CONGRESS WAS GIVEN A 57-PAGE
government report it had requested on the Economic Development Administration. The report strongly criticized EDA as an ineffective,
poorly funded, mismanaged attempt to combat unemployment and economic hardship within the states and localities. Congress chose to ignore
the report and approved a two-year extension of EDA with a total authorization of more than $1.4 billion. (As usual Congress did not follow
up on its promise, and appropriated a total of $258.5 million for fiscal
1975.)

The little-noticed study* came to be called the "Bellmon Report"
because it was an amendment by Sen. Henry Bellmon (R.-Okla.)
that requested the six-month review by the Office of Management and

---

* "Report to the Congress on the Proposal for an Economic Adjustment Program,"
referred to in the previous chapter.

Budget and the Commerce Department. It concluded that the EDA—which has spent hundreds of millions of tax dollars since its beginning in 1966—was "inadequate in pursuing" its objectives.

EDA was created in 1965 under the Public Works and Economic Development Act. Its program included public works grants and loans, business loans and loan guarantees, and technical, planning, and research assistance aimed at economic redevelopment of specific areas suffering from chronic unemployment.

Beginning in 1966 EDA found that 424 areas of the country were eligible for assistance solely on the basis of heavy unemployment. In fiscal 1973 there were 427 areas qualified on the same basis. But of the 424 areas of substantial unemployment in fiscal 1966, 311 of these areas still had serious unemployment as of 1974.

In a massively understated conclusion in the face of such devastating statistics, the "Bellmon Report" said these figures "could indicate that the programs of EDA have made only minimal progress toward the original objective of creating employment in areas of persistent, high unemployment."

One of the reasons for its obvious ineffectiveness, the study said, was that EDA's financial resources have been dispersed "in relatively small amounts to a large number of areas. Over the years of its existence, the EDA funds have been distributed to about 1,300 separate areas.

"With but a few exceptions, the amount of assistance to any one area has not been great enough to overcome the economic causes of distress in the area and, therefore, has not resulted in self-sustaining economic growth sufficient to eliminate the problem." For example, the study found that about 65 percent of EDA's funding went for public works projects while only 18 percent went for direct assistance to the private sector. Significantly, it concluded (brace yourself) that the private sector was "the principal determinant" in an area's economic development.

EDA's policy of spreading out its resources over hundreds of localities, many of them small communities, was in most respects regarded as a waste of money. Over one-third of its public works funds went to communities with less than 2,500 people, over half to towns whose populations were less than 5,000. "There are relatively few kinds of economic activities which can operate efficiently in such small communities, so the potential for economic development in the communities is relatively small," the report said.

One middle-level EDA official, who did not wish to be identified, told me, "Too often we've put money into a town when it would be better if the town went away. They're small communities with dwindling populations, one-industry towns with little basis for future economic development. They would be better left, in many instances, to the fate of normal market conditions."

The Bellmon study also found that state officials, who most likely have a better grasp of the economic conditions and needs of their communities than does Washington, have little or no role in determining priorities in EDA's sprinkler-system allocation of grants. Moreover, the report found that "because state and local officials are unable to predict how much EDA assistance they might receive, they are often unable to effectively plan for the use of the EDA funds."

EDA has probably placed too much emphasis on public works funding because Congress in recent years has gone bananas over the concept of public works employment, believing it to be the cure-all for curbing unemployment. Also, much of the public works assistance has been provided with the idea that it would build the economic "infrastructure" desired by businesses wishing to locate or expand in a given area. "But often businesses have not responded to such indirect incentives," said the Bellmon study. Moreover, EDA seldom followed up its grant-giving to determine what other incentives could be provided to businesses to lure them into a particular depressed area. "Some evaluations indicate," the report said, "that *direct incentives to the private sector result in a higher return on investment in terms of jobs per dollar than do public works*." That sentence says more about how to deal with depressed areas and persistent unemployment than anything Congress has heard before or since. Unless one is talking about massive federal programs involving billions of dollars in public works jobs, which would only feed the deficit and further drive up inflation, it is the private sector—the free marketplace—that offers America a better investment employmentwise over the long haul. There are many approaches open to government to help business obtain working capital to provide needed jobs. EDA, according to the most extensive evaluation available, is not one of them.

21

Coast Guard Selected Reserve Program

$27.9 Million

THE U.S. COAST GUARD SAYS IT NEEDS this program and that its termination would lessen the effectiveness of the service's responsibilities. However, President Nixon, presumably with the consent of his military advisers, said abolishing the reserve program "would not significantly reduce the overall effectiveness of the Coast Guard."

Nixon proposed terminating the Selected Reserve in 1970 but Congress ignored the idea. The Coast Guard argues strongly for retaining the reservists. However, the evidence is persuasive that the program could be terminated without really affecting the Coast Guard's work in any substantive way.

There were 11,700 men in the Selected Reserve as of June 1974. After serving two years' active duty, Coastguardmen are required to enter the reserves and train one weekend a month plus put in two weeks of active duty each year for which they are paid.

But the Coast Guard also has 10,402 men in the Ready Reserves, or so-called voluntary reserves. These men have had four full years of training and experience in the guard and are kept on a volunteer, non-paid, standby basis. Thus, this force would be ready to serve in peace-time or wartime emergencies, despite termination of the Selected Reserve.

Occasionally the Coast Guard has called up the Selected Reserves for emergency duty but the numbers used are usually small. For example, as of late 1974 the last callup involved 134 men in the spring of 1973 during the Mississippi floods. But the Ready Reserves have also been called up, such as when tornadoes struck Louisville.

In fiscal 1975 the Selected Reserve Program was funded at more than $27.9 million. The Coast Guard maintains that it uses the Selected Reserves to augment regular personnel at some of its facilities because Congress has not provided it with enough funds to handle numerous jobs it has been assigned. But by June 1974 the Coast Guard had an author-ized military strength, not including reservists, of 36,730 men plus a ci-vilian force of 6,283. Its funding for fiscal 1975 was almost $879.6 million.

Complaints by the Coast Guard of inadequate funding may be jus-tified, for Congress has through the years piled on the service a number of programs, including oil spill cleanups, bridge construction, boating safety assistance, and other projects. But the question of whether the U.S. Coast Guard itself should be better funded should not preclude dis-mantling a costly yet low-priority reserve program that in peacetime would be better off on standby status. Of course, Selected Reservists could be transferred into the voluntary Ready Reserves and thereby be available to the Coast Guard for any emergencies.

22

Military Servants

$5.4 Million

OUT OF THE GAMUT OF GOVERNMENT WASTE and extravagance there is nothing more outrageous and arrogant than the use of enlisted men by the military brass as their personal servants.

Pentagon regulations, through loophole-ridden language, allow generals and admirals to use enlisted servicemen as their servants. Their jobs include work as valets, social secretaries, cooks, waiters, errand runners, cabin boys, grocery shoppers, babysitters, housemaids, chauffeurs, lawn keepers, and bartenders at parties—all paid for by the taxpayer. There are laws that prohibit using enlisted men as servants but broadly worded military regulations allow U.S. servicemen to be used for virtually every imaginable task.

Senator Proxmire has been the leading congressional critic of this 18th-century practice. The Senate voted 73-9 in 1973 to cut the number of allowable servants from 1,722 to 218. That figure, however, was subsequently raised by the House to 675—the limit as of 1974 (the Senate has voted three times to reduce the figure to 218 but the House has refused to go along in conference).

The 675 military servants are parceled out to 450 of America's highest-ranking generals and admirals. The Army chief of staff, the chairman of the Joint Chiefs of Staff, the chief of naval operations, the commandant of the Marine Corps, and the Air Force chief of staff are given five servants each. Thirteen other Army generals, eight admirals, one Marine Corps general, and 14 Air Force generals receive three servants each. The remainder of the 450 top brass have to struggle along with one or two servants each, with the exception of the superintendent of the U.S. Naval Academy, who is given four.

Most of the military servants are based in the Washington, D.C., area—at least 189—with the remaining number performing a broad range of servants' chores at military posts throughout the country and around the world.

The $5.4 million cost of providing servants to America's top military officers is figured on the basis of an average $8,000 annual GI salary times the 675 servants allowed. It is a very conservative figure and does not include the cost of military training, benefits, and other expenses that would not have to be borne if the practice were outlawed completely. Moreover, it is believed that there are actually hundreds of additional servicemen beyond the authorized 675 who are used to perform servile duties.

Largely as a result of publicity focused on the use of military servants, the Pentagon in August 1974 issued new regulations covering the use of enlisted volunteers for domestic chores. Deputy Defense Secretary William Clements said in a directive that "the propriety of such duties is governed by the official purpose which they serve, rather than the nature of the duties." Senator Proxmire called Clements' rationale for such duties "an example of aristocratic arrogance." He said it provided generals and admirals with the use of servants "in military clothing. This is an intolerable situation and is a disgrace to the armed services."

Clements' directive said enlisted aides were authorized to relieve generals and admirals "of those minor tasks and details which, if performed by the officers, would be at the expense of the officers' primary military and official duties."

The new regulations listed five categories of work that enlisted aides could be ordered to do:

- "Assist with the care, cleanliness and order of assigned quarters, uniforms and military personal equipment"
- "Perform as point of contact in the officers' quarters. Receive and maintain records of telephone calls, make appointments and receive guests and visitors"
- "Assist in the planning, preparation, arrangement and conduct of official social functions and activities, such as receptions, parties and dinners"
- "Assist in purchasing, preparing and serving food and beverages in the general and flag officer's assigned quarters"
- "Accomplish tasks which aid the officer in the performance of his military and official responsibilities, including performing errands for the officer, providing security for the quarters and providing administrative assistance"

The directive's language, obviously, provides regulation loopholes through which almost any type of job can be turned over, by superiors, to GI "slaves." Indeed, a General Accounting Office investigation found that two-thirds of the Marine servants were black and 98 percent of the Navy's stewards Filipinos. The GAO also discovered that at least $1 million alone had been spent by the Nixon administration to pay for GI servants assigned to the White House. Ninety-one Navy stewards—almost all Filipinos—were assigned to perform various servant chores while an additional 65 Navy aides chauffeured White House staffers, the watchdog agency found. GI servants were also assigned to Camp David, the presidential retreat, as well as to Nixon's estates at San Clemente and Key Biscayne and the presidential yacht *Sequoia*. The stewards did everything from cleaning up the cabins at Camp David to washing dishes in the White House staff mess, and even working without pay as butlers at private parties in the homes of White House officials.

The practice of using military servicemen and stewards at the taxpayers' expense to perform domestic chores for our nation's top brass, not to mention the White House, is a travesty. Army Secretary Robert Froehlke, in a weak defense of some of these practices before House Appropriations Committee Chairman George Mahon, said he didn't think his chief of staff should have to rush home after work to mow his lawn. Snapped Mahon, "Well, he could hire his own help like the rest of us."

Most Americans cook their own meals, pick up their own laundry, clean their own homes, and drive themselves to and from work. Our military men can do the same or—at their more than adequate salaries—hire their own help.

At a time when the all-volunteer Army is being put to the ultimate test to determine whether America's fighting force can be maintained through a nondraft system without weakening one of the strongest military powers in the world, the GI servant system is degrading and humiliating to the U.S. serviceman. The American taxpayer will gladly pay the taxes to maintain our military strength at the level needed to keep our nation free. But continuation of the present aristocratic practice of using servicemen as a pool for military domestics can only further weaken popular support for America's already highly criticized military budget.

23

Federal Costs of Grading, Classing, and Inspecting Tobacco, Cotton, and Grain

$16.4 Million

THE AGRICULTURE DEPARTMENT, AS IT does for many agricultural industries, grades, classes, and inspects cotton, tobacco, and grain. But while other agricultural industries pay the cost of these government services, cotton, tobacco, and a major share of the grain industries do not. These costs are picked up by the taxpayer.

The annual costs for government grading, classing, and inspecting in fiscal 1975 were estimated at $8.5 million for cotton, $3.2 million for certain grains, and $4.7 million for tobacco. If payment from these three industries were recovered to the government, the taxpayer would save a total of $16.4 million.

It would seem only fair and equitable that since the poultry, dairy, fruit, and vegetable industries pay the cost of these government services, the cotton-tobacco-grain industries do the same. This would take legislation. Getting such legislation through Congress in the face of opposition from members who states grow cotton, tobacco, or grains (not to mention some powerful committee chairmen, too) would be like moving Mount Sinai to Beverly Hills.

Even so, abolishing what is in effect a gift to three powerful industries, with equally powerful friends in Congress, would be a nice gift to the taxpayers.

24

Office of Juvenile Delinquency

$381.5 Million

NO ONE CAN ARGUE WITH THE FACT THAT juvenile delinquency is a serious crime problem in the United States today. But one can legitimately argue against the need to establish a new bureaucracy within the federal government to deal with the vast multiplicity of juvenile delinquency problems.

Congress passed legislation in August 1974 to create a new Office of Juvenile Delinquency within the Justice Department's Law Enforcement Assistance Administration (LEAA). The bill authorized appropriations of $75 million for fiscal 1975, $125 million for fiscal 1976, and $150 million for fiscal 1977, a total of $350 million over a three-year period. This was in addition to over $140 million already being spent annually by LEAA on various juvenile delinquency programs.

The legislation also authorized $10.5 million for each of the three years to provide temporary shelters and counseling services around the country for runaway youths.

Now, on any list of priorities for America, shelters for runaway children has to rank relatively low. First, runaways are not necessarily delinquents. Second, even strong proponents of the new agency conceded there were no firm data or accurate statistics to gauge how serious or how broad the problem of runaway youths is nationally. There have been studies indicating that perhaps as high as 90 percent of all runaways return home within the first week. Sponsors of the bill said one million kids ran away from home annually. But social workers who testified said the number was half that amount, though they conceded they were only estimating. In other words, the evidence is not there to justify the expenditure of $31.5 million to build places for runaways to stay. No doubt it is a problem but it is one that should be left to the localities to deal with and not Washington.

Under the core of the program, funds are allocated to the states on the basis of their youth population, with a minimum allocation of $200,000 per state. The law requires participating states to establish a juvenile delinquency prevention and treatment program with direct funding of local programs to be authorized by the federal administrator. The program also established a Coordinating Council on Juvenile Justice and Delinquency Prevention, an Institute of Juvenile Justice and Delinquency Prevention, an Institute of Corrections, and an Advisory Committee for Juvenile Justice and Delinquency Prevention.

All of this was established by Congress in the face of LEAA's ongoing antijuvenile delinquency efforts, which totaled over $300 million between 1969 and 1974. In addition, HEW had since 1968 been operating the Youth Development and Delinquency Prevention Administration, which, like LEAA, operated a program of grants designed to help states and localities to improve their juvenile systems and to provide diagnostic, treatment, rehabilitation, and prevention services to delinquent youths. But the HEW program always failed to seek its full authorization from Congress (which is like a slap in the face to Congress) and consistently spent less than it received. It expired in fiscal 1974.

A study by a federal interdepartmental council seeking to coordinate all juvenile delinquency activities in the government found that some $12 billion was allocated in fiscal 1972 alone for a broad range of youth development and juvenile delinquency programs. The programs ran the gamut from the Labor Department's Job Corps to the Office of Education's dropout prevention program to the Agriculture Department's 4-H program for the inner-city poor to the Interior Department's Youth Conservation Corps to the Drug Abuse Prevention program to the Bureau of Indian Affairs program for delinquents, to name only a few. In other words, the youth of America were hardly being ignored.

Still, there can be no doubt that juvenile delinquency is a severe problem in America—almost one-half of all serious crimes are committed by youths under the age of 18. But over the past several years LEAA has been pouring about $140 million annually into the states through grants, with the states providing up to 50 percent in matching funds. A Justice Department official who worked closely on developing the new LEAA program and supports it had to admit that under the original grant program, "LEAA has put a substantial amount into juvenile delinquency. There's no doubt about it." And its programs—similar to its broader anticrime assistance—were a sound and valid approach, providing the states with the resources to deal with the local peculiarities of juvenile delinquency in their own way. Obviously, juvenile delinquency problems in Boston are not like juvenile delinquency problems in Fort Lauderdale.

There is room for serious doubt whether a new bureaucracy in Washington can deal with the problem more effectively than can locally run administrations that know their needs firsthand. In fact, the aforementioned Justice Department official told me he would have liked to maintain the original LEAA grant program without all the bureaucratic trappings added by Congress. "There's a good case for it," he said of the old program. Congress, however, opted for the trappings.

Whatever administrative overhead the new Office of Juvenile Delinquency will have—perhaps as high as seven percent of the overall budget—there will be that much less that could go to the states to deal with and help prevent juvenile delinquency.

When President Ford signed the bill into law he said he would not ask for full funding of the new program because "the economic situation demands across-the-board restraint, especially in the federal budget." He said spending would be held to the levels already being provided for juvenile delinquency. Congress will no doubt have other ideas when it comes to appropriating its promised authorization of $381.5 million over three years. Meantime, that is the spending figure Congress and President Ford put into law and one we must accept as tentatively valid.

With juvenile delinquency on the rise, there is a very good case for increasing LEAA funds for block and categorical grants. But that increased support should be without the new office, administrator, council, advisory committee, and institutes, if Washington is effectively and efficiently to reach America's delinquent youths many miles away.

25

Renegotiation Board

$5.1 Million

THE PURPOSE OF THE RENEGOTIATION BOARD
is to eliminate excess profits made by corporations through defense contracts with the government. The figures indicate the board has not been
doing its job. The profit rate of return for many top firms doing business
with the Pentagon has skyrocketed. The board should be abolished.

The board is supposed to be a watchdog for the taxpayers, giving
careful scrutiny to a contractor's profits for the fiscal year. If the five-
member board determines the profits to be excessive, that portion considered excessively above a reasonable rate of return must be returned to
the government.

In 1973, after renegotiation of their profit rates, the board allowed
Grumman Aircraft to keep a 76 percent profit return, Dow Chemical
Company 48 percent, and Norris Industries, Inc. 77 percent on contracts
they had with the government. According to Senator Proxmire, there

were cases where one or two small firms were allowed profits of more than 1,000 percent after renegotiation.

Even those most sympathetic to the plight of industry in today's sagging market must concede that these "after-renegotiation profit rates" are excessively high—higher than profit rates normally associated with similar industry production.

The board's record in recent years on excess profits has been dismal when one considers the tens of billions of dollars spent each year on defense procurement and the high profit rate many contractors—though not all—have made.

In 1971 the board got back $65.2 million in excess profits, $40.2 million in 1972, $28 million in 1973, and about $70 million in fiscal 1974. Compare these profits in an inflated economy with excess profits obtained by the board during the post-Korean War period: $167 million in 1955, $152.6 million in 1956, and $151 million in 1957.

Under the Renegotiation Act of 1951, which established the present board, companies doing work in excess of $1 million in any fiscal year must file reports with the board. The board's requirements are applicable to contracts with the Departments of Defense, Army, Navy, and Air Force, the Maritime Administration, the General Services Administration, the Atomic Energy Commission, the National Aeronautics and Space Administration, and the Federal Aviation Administration.

The old board was swept out of office by President Nixon and its present makeup consists primarily of political appointments who serve at the pleasure of the President.

The renegotiation function should clearly continue perhaps under some other independent agency, such as the General Accounting Office with its superior auditing staff. But the board is obviously ill equipped to deal with the nation's rising defense costs. Even with its two regional boards working as a clearinghouse, the board's staff of less than 200 cannot begin to cope with the amount of defense prime contract awards, which totaled $36.9 billion in fiscal 1973. "It is not possible for an agency with such a small staff to keep up with the workload indicated by the figures for defense contract awards and the large number of filings," the Senate Appropriations Committee said in a report.

A full-fledged study of the board was under way in late 1974 but many in Congress believe the best course of action is to get rid of the board and pass on its work to some existing and more competent agency.

Ideally, the procurement agencies themselves should bear the full responsibility for preventing excess profits and be given the right to renegotiate contracts if necessary. Cost overruns in the billions have obviously gotten out of control on many military procurement programs and, under stern congressional oversight, the buck must stop with the military agencies themselves.

26

Overseas Private Investment Corporation

IN PORT-AU-PRINCE, HAITI, BEHIND A high stonewall sits the two-century-old Habitation Leclerc, once the resplendent residence of Napoleon's sister, Pauline Leclerc. Now a pleasure dome resort for the wealthy, it offers everything from huge circular mattresses, large sunken baths, and private swimming pools, to a discotheque and all the food and liquor you can consume for $150 a day per couple. "Since the Garden of Eden there has never been a place like Habitation Leclerc . . . elegant, exotic, erotic. Privacy within a lush exciting garden of pleasure," its advertising boasts.

The owners of the Leclerc hotel resort were able to open the Caribbean hideaway in January 1974 with the help of a $415,000 loan from the U.S. government's Overseas Private Investment Corporation (OPIC).

Congress approved OPIC in 1969 to take over and expand upon various insurance and loan-guarantee programs previously run by the

Agency for International Development (AID) for U.S. investors abroad. Since that time OPIC has written billions of dollars' worth of policies insuring major American corporations investing in developing countries against the risks of war, expropriation of property, and currency inconvertibility.

In effect, the United States has been subsidizing some of America's biggest corporations to send their capital abroad at a time when unemployment and a money-starved U.S. capital market require just the opposite. The Senate Foreign Relations Committee found that 79 percent of all OPIC-issued insurance was provided to firms on *Fortune* magazine's list of 500 largest corporations and 50 largest banks.

By far OPIC's biggest function is its political-risk insurance program, with a total of about $3.5 to $4 billion in liabilities outstanding in 1974, which of course the U.S. Treasury would have to honor in the event those policies came due. OPIC's guaranteed loans and direct loans—like the one made to the Habitation Leclerc—constitute a much smaller share of its overall program. Its portfolio of guaranteed development loans consisted in early 1974 of 23 projects totaling $200 million.

OPIC's five-year authority was to have expired by the end of 1974 but Congress decided to extend its authority for an additional three years until the end of 1977 with the proviso that it turn over its entire insurance program to private insurance firms within that period. Moreover, Congress ordered that by the end of 1979 all of OPIC's remaining programs must be turned over to AID or dissolved with the single exception of its reinsurance function, which would allow the agency to issue reinsurance to private insurance agencies for a percentage of their potential losses.

OPIC's last congressional appropriation, $25 million, came in fiscal 1974 and therefore no operational amount would be listed as an amount saved if the agency were totally abolished as of fiscal 1975. Congress turned down a request for an additional $25 million for fiscal 1975. Yet its political-risk insurance liabilities and guaranteed loans could indeed cost taxpayers a fortune if pending claims against OPIC were successful. It should be noted, too, that since 1969 OPIC has received more than $200 million in congressional appropriations.

As pointed out in the Senate Foreign Relations Committee's report, "OPIC's financial viability is in doubt and it may well have to rely on congressional appropriations or Treasury payments based on the full faith and credit clause of OPIC's authorizing legislation to bail it out."

The committee also found that if OPIC had not received $81.2 million in appropriations since the 1970 fiscal year, "it would currently have only $58,250,000 in its insurance reserves instead of $139,500,000." The committee concluded that OPIC's "precarious financial position becomes even more clear when its earned reserves [that is, reserves minus appropriations] are contrasted with outstanding claims and guarantees."

OPIC is an unnecessary and costly government program that could end up costing taxpayers billions of dollars. At the beginning of 1974 there were currently outstanding against OPIC some $369 million in unsettled claims* and guarantees** against total insurance reserves of $146.5 million. The two largest claims—$92.5 million by ITT and $154 million by Anaconda—arose from the Chilean expropriations. In fact, all but about $8 million of some $100 million in outstanding guarantees were as a result of Chilean expropriations.

The committee further concluded: "If the pending ITT and Anaconda arbitrations . . . heavily favor the companies, OPIC could easily find itself deeply in the red."

The federal government should not be in the insurance-writing business. In fact, experts maintain that over three-fourths of investments by U.S. firms in lesser-developed countries are uninsured because the companies say they don't need such protection. Furthermore, the great bulk of the corporations receiving this tax-subsidized insurance protection are the giants of U.S. industry and more than financially able to purchase their own insurance from the private sector. Despite the trend to provide a host of government guarantees, loans, and other emoluments for business, the fact remains that business must survive or perish within the free market system. Also, it has never been adequately demonstrated that U.S. corporations investing in foreign countries are always beneficial to less-developed countries. John Sagan, vice president and treasurer of Ford Motor Company, and William Meehan, assistant treasurer of Mo-

---

* Claims on OPIC are amounts, it argues, it does not have to pay and the dispute must be settled in arbitration.

** Guarantees are amounts that expropriating governments agreed to pay and that OPIC will pay if the expropriating government defaults.

torola, both testified that there was no intrinsic requirement that OPIC-insured companies purchase U.S. products. Further, both testified that OPIC encourages an outward flow of capital from the United States by encouraging industries to invest abroad, and that OPIC in fact, at least in the short run, contributes to a worsening of America's balance-of-payments problem.

Thus, the committee concluded that OPIC's investment guarantee program was "at best, only a marginal contributor to the development of the poorer countries of the world and OPIC is only a marginal stimulus to private investment in less developed countries."

Congress made the wrong decision when it decided to phase out OPIC's corporate insurance program over such a long period of time and to continue with a program of reinsurance for private insurance companies that agree to pick up OPIC policies. It should be phased out entirely and much sooner than five years.

Clifford P. Case, Republican senator from New Jersey, for one, agrees we should abolish OPIC entirely: "The suggestions made by the majority for a gradual shift of OPIC's insurance to private industry, with what I believe would be an open-ended reinsurance commitment by the United States, are in my opinion unrealistic and would not in my judgment accomplish the majority's stated purpose.

"I believe strongly that the only way to terminate the program is to terminate it."

Amen.

27

President's Commission on Productivity and Work Quality

$2 Million

THE NAME OF THIS COMMISSION MIGHT JUST as well be the President's Commission on the Quality of Bathroom Plungers and Ice Cube Trays. Its purpose would be equally ludicrous.

When the House passed legislation on May 10, 1974, extending the life of this commission through the 1975 fiscal year, H. R. Gross (R.-Iowa) called it "a boondoggle." As usual, the venerable fiscal watchdog was right on target.

The commission has been around for four years, though it's difficult to find anyone in Congress who can tell you anything of value it has done to justify total expenditures of $5.5 million since its inception in 1970. Predictably, the House report accompanying the bill extending the commission's life did not provide one example of its own productivity and work quality, let alone anyone else's. Originally its sponsors sought a $5-million authorization but the House defeated that, settling instead for half that amount after Gross suggested to his colleagues, "We can find better places than this to spend $5 million, can't we?" (This was reduced to $2 million in conference with both houses.)

"They haven't accomplished anything of a tangible nature," Gross said. "We have councils and advisory boards running out of our ears in this government."

The commission's purpose ostensibly is to "promote the productivity of the American economy and to improve worker morale and the quality of work." It has three primary means to implement these objectives: (1) creation of labor-management productivity councils of the World War II type; (2) research projects; and (3) public information programs.

The House Banking Committee, which approved the commission's renewal and original $5-million request, said in a report that efforts to "help improve the quality of working life are justified regardless of whether there are any immediate discernible results in terms of productivity increases." In other words, the commission doesn't even have to obtain any actual results in pursuit of its most tangible purpose—productivity.

During House debate on extending the life of the commission, some members said they supported the agency because of work it had done in California to speed the shipments of fruits and vegetables to markets. Its supporters, needless to say, were all from California.

Seeing the agency for what it is, Henry Gonzalez, Democratic representative from Texas, called it "just another government employment service. It hasn't done one study . . . to warrant extending its life." The congressman recalled the commission had once studied the water content of tomatoes, made a study of transportation, and examined the productivity of hospitals. But he rightly noted that the government has enormous departments already concerned with these problems. Even the House Banking Committee's report questioned the "usefulness of some of the commission's proposed projects . . . dealing with such concerns as banking, restaurants, and education."

Worker morale and work quality? Productivity? Aren't these why we have a Labor Department and a Commerce Department? The commission's work is simply duplicating what other agencies are already set up to do.

But the bottom-line argument is of course that America doesn't need a commission to tell it how to be productive. Productivity rises from the workings of a sound economy in which capital investment and expansion are allowed to thrive. Worker morale and work quality will improve when workers find that less of the fruit of their labors goes toward paying local, state, and federal taxes and more of their sweat goes into lining their own pockets with the rewards of the free market system. Unfortunately, the reverse seems to be true today. Perhaps a commission on how this trend can be turned around would be money better spent. In the meantime, this bureaucratic hangnail should be clipped.

28

Alaska Railroad

$6.2 Million

"IT IS TIME FOR THE FEDERAL GOVERNMENT to get out of the operation and ownership of the Alaska Railroad."

That's what President Nixon said to Congress in a 1970 message outlining proposals to terminate or reduce 57 government programs he believed of low priority, in need of basic reform, or obsolete.

Congress never acted on the President's proposals, which would have saved a whopping $2.5 billion. His proposal to sell the Alaska Railroad remains a good one.

The government railroad provides passenger and freight service ostensibly to stimulate settlement and industrial and agricultural development of Alaska. The railroad's 470.3-mile main line extends from Seward and Whittier through Anchorage to Fairbanks and includes branch lines to Eielson Air Force Base and to the Matanuska and Suntrana coal fields.

Congress appropriated over $6.2 million for payment to the Alaska

Railroad Revolving Fund for capital improvements for fiscal 1975. It is money the taxpayers could just as well have saved if the railroad was privately owned.

With the discovery of tremendous oil resources in Alaska and the region's potential for economic development, the need for maintaining federal ownership of the rail line has vanished. The Alaska Railroad has obviously become an attractive investment and should be sold either to the state of Alaska or to private enterprise.

29

Revenue Sharing

$16 Billion

IT IS SAID THAT WHEN CONGRESS PASSED revenue sharing it truly took leave of its senses.

In 1972 Americans were paying well in excess of $20 billion annually just to pay the interest on the federal debt, which was even then approaching $500 billion. But that year Congress, blissfully oblivious to this financial mess, decided to give away $30.2 billion over five years to the states and localities.

The "revenue sharing" title is a publicity agent's dream. It conveys all the good things: charity, concern for the plight of local government, generosity. But one thing was wrong. The government had no money to share. It was in debt and it was sinking deeper into debt. The money that was to go into revenue sharing had to be borrowed if it was to be "shared." It was almost laughable if it were not so pitifully sad.

Its supporters readily admitted at the time that $6 billion a year wouldn't make much of a dent in the financial plight of the nation's states and thousands of local governments. Once begun it would have to be increased and increased . . .

"Chicken feed" was the way Democratic Congressman George H. Mahon of Texas described it. "That is a mere pittance of what it will become once it is begun," the chairman of the powerful House Appropriations Committee warned his colleagues. ". . . if you grasp this tiger by the tail, you will find it difficult to turn him loose. Never in this century would you ever turn that tiger loose, and everyone here knows it."

Mayors and governors descended on Congress with greedy fury to press for approval of the program, which owned the blessing of President Nixon, who saw in it some redemption for an obviously weak domestic program. House Ways and Means Committee Chairman Wilbur Mills was dead set against it and vowed it would never get past his committee alive. But the Democrat from Arkansas came down with a severe case of presidential fever that year and quickly changed his tune. The revenue-sharing formula was clearly devised to appeal to the great bulk of rural states and thus was assured of the majority votes needed for passage, despite an unsuccessful attempt by urban state representatives to substitute a formula weighted toward their constituencies.

The idea for revenue sharing has been kicking around ever since Democratic economist Walter Heller conceived it in the early 1960s, when it appeared that the federal tax structure would generate a revenue surplus. That possibility quickly evaporated, however, with Lyndon Johnson's Great Society spending binge. Richard Nixon's deficits made a surplus even more remote. The average federal deficit during the 1960s was about $10 billion a year, while in the first four fiscal years of Nixon's administration, the federal deficit averaged about $28 billion per year. During this four-year period, as a result of borrowing to pay for the government's spending, the debt rose more than $110 billion. Nonetheless, the Congress went ahead and happily approved revenue sharing.

In 1972 (before revenue sharing), the federal government gave away $37 billion in grants to the states and localities, providing them with 21 percent of their total revenues. Yet still the mayors and governors trooped to Washington pleading that this was not enough. Supposedly, $5-$6 billion more a year, doled out among almost 38,000 state and local governments, would make a difference in their financial status.

105

Despite its passage by Congress and approval by President Nixon in an election year, there were ominous warnings by a few lonely voices. Surprisingly, Wisconsin's Democratic Senator Gaylord Nelson, who religiously supports virtually every social welfare bill, said, "We come now then to the real gut question that no one wants to talk about— Where in the hell do we get the money to pay for it?"

Nelson, whose votes have contributed, perhaps more than any other senator's, to the federal deficit, said that revenue sharing—without the necessary taxes to support it—was "fiscally irresponsible." Moreover, he argued, "Those who spend the money ought to have the responsibility of raising the taxes."

Democratic leader Mike Mansfield, another faithful Senate liberal who opposed revenue sharing, told me he still opposes it because he dislikes the precedent-breaking step of Congress authorizing and appropriating money simultaneously. He also frowns on giving away so much money "without some quid pro quo such as requiring matching funds, supervision of the money's use, and congressional oversight.

"I am concerned also," continued Mansfield in the interview, "about some of the uses the money is being put to, building bridle paths, and the like—a lot of things like that which I think are questionable.* This is given out with a lavish hand. I'd rather see the money used to decrease the national debt . . . that would have a tremendous psychological effect on the economy along with cuts in the budget."

Even Edmund S. Muskie, Democratic senator from Maine and one of the original promoters of revenue sharing, has conceded that one of the chief problems is that it gives money "to more than 38,000 jurisdictions, some of which have neither demonstrated a need nor provided a use for it. In the spirit of compromise necessary to secure passage of the act, the program was transformed into a streamlined form of federal aid to virtually every local government in the nation—regardless of size, function or relative need."

Nelson's argument concerning responsibility for raising taxes is a particularly strong one. The entire system of revenue sharing destroys the concept of accountability. Our federal bureaucracy raises the money through taxes and borrowing in order to give it away to local govern-

---

* Some of the more questionable ones included a pooltable in the Alaskan village of Venetie and plans for at least two municipal golf courses.

ments but has no say as to how the money is spent. Those on the local level who spend the funds do so by avoiding responsibility for raising needed revenue.

Thus, revenue sharing represents one big copout for state and local officials who have spent their governments into the red but fear the political consequences of either raising taxes or telling their constituents that cutbacks are needed. If the federal government can bail them out, they're home scot-free. Each state and local government must be responsible to its citizens for taxing and spending those taxes prudently for needed government programs.

On the other hand, Congress must also be able to resist pleas from the states for no-strings-attached revenue. If revenue is so badly needed, then the voters would surely approve the taxes to raise it. If the people will not approve such increased taxation, then it is reasonable to assume they are quite willing to do without certain programs, or reduce those programs they can no longer afford.

Congress caved in to the political demands of the cities and states—particularly the large urban giants—and agreed to do what the states and localities would not: borrow the money at high interest rates and, in effect, pay the ransom under dire threats of political retribution.

It was in 1972 when Congress embarked on its five-year $30.2-billion escapade. But as of fiscal 1975 almost $16 billion in federal funds could have been saved if Congress had so resolved through the appropriate legislation permanently to suspend the entire program. Under the remaining revenue-sharing plan, $6.2 billion was to be distributed in fiscal 1975, $6.35 billion in fiscal 1976, and $3.3 billion for the first six months of fiscal 1977.

With Congress' new budget-control committees searching about for ways to cut billions of dollars, the remaining billions of revenue sharing would be an appropriate place to start. It would result in no substantial loss in jobs, affect no industries, but would relieve the mounting federal deficit of a gargantuan burden. State and local bureaucrats would no doubt howl at the thought of losing this new pipeline to Washington's coffers, but the American taxpayers would heave a sigh of relief. If the states and localities so desperately need additional revenue they can surely raise it on their own far more cheaply than the federal government with its enormous overhead and bureaucracy. Congress should have the courage honestly to announce, "There is nothing to share. Our Treasury is in debt."

30

Legal Services

$190 Million

AFTER A FIERCE THREE-YEAR BATTLE OVER legislation to establish a Legal Services Corporation, President Nixon in July 1974 signed the bitterly fought bill into law while he was on the brink of being impeached by the House and convicted by the Senate. Weeks later he resigned.

Many in Congress who strongly opposed this program believe that had Nixon not been under the incredible pressure of impeachment, he would have vetoed the bill as he did in 1971.

The corps of Legal Services attorneys to aid the poor, since its inception in 1966 under Lyndon Johnson's tragically deceptive antipoverty program, has been in the vanguard of "social activist" battles. The poverty lawyers have lobbied in behalf of legislation, worked to overturn state and national laws, and aided partisan political organizations—all at the taxpayers' expense.

The law prohibits federal funds from being used by government-supported programs to lobby in behalf of issues under congressional consideration. The statute reads: "No part of the money appropriated by any enactment of Congress shall, in the absence of express authorization by Congress, be used directly or indirectly, to pay for any personal service advertisement, telegram, telephone, letter, printed or written matter, or other device, intended or designed to influence in any manner a member of Congress, whether before or after the introduction of any bill. . . ."

Yet despite this prohibition, Legal Services programs have been expending public funds to lobby for legislation—particularly for the very bill reestablishing their program under an independent corporation. Under the legislation, Legal Services was shifted from the dismantled Office of Economic Opportunity (OEO) to a new independent public corporation run by an 11-member board named by the President. Congress authorized $90 million for the 1975 fiscal year and $100 million for the 1976 fiscal year.

Many conservatives opposed the bill because it contained authority for the new corporation to finance outside "backup centers." These centers, at 15 universities and law schools, had been getting about $5 million a year in grants and contracts to undertake legal research upon which a wide variety of class action and social activist suits were based. Liberals agreed to remove this authority from the measure in order to soothe conservative opposition and win Nixon's approval. But it remained evident to the bill's strongest opponents that the corporation still possessed the authority to contract for similar legal research from other sources, such as so-called public interest law firms.

Rejecting a proposal to shift Legal Services to the states under a block grant approach, Nixon decided in 1971 to establish the poverty attorneys under an independent corporation. He vetoed one version in December 1971. A similar bill died in conference in 1972. Finally, in 1974 the bill was signed into law by an all-but-destroyed President.

If the history of Legal Services provides any clue to its future, the so-called antipoverty lawyers will continue to be a tax-supported corps of young, politically liberal attorneys eager to place their ideological stamp upon legislation or to overturn existing statutes they deem anathema to their political and social philosophy. For if anything is clear, it is that Legal Services groups have for years been using federal funds to promote legislation in obvious violation of the law. For example, Action for

Legal Rights (ALR), an organization of law school deans and lawyers that lobbied strongly for the independent corporation bill, has received contributions from legal-aid programs financed by the Office of Economic Opportunity.* Groups that have given money to the ALR include the Legal Aid Society of Cleveland, California Rural Legal Assistance, Poverty Lawyers for Effective Advocacy, and Lawyers Committee to Save Legal Services.

Howard Phillips, the former OEO director who studied Legal Services from the inside, wrote this about its activities: "The brazenness with which Legal Services attorneys flout the antilobby law is overwhelming, yet there have been no special prosecutors called to deal with it, no special Senate or House investigations [or even oversight]. . . ."

Mickey Kantor, a former official of Legal Services under President Nixon and erstwhile executive director of ALR, stated candidly once what Legal Services is all about: "With all its benefits, litigation remains expensive, time consuming, often frustrating. . . . Similarly, litigation can be dysfunctional in terms of building organizational strength among the poor. . . . Legislative advocacy has always been encouraged by OEO. There has never been a ruling that Legal Services must be invited to appear before a legislative committee as a precondition to participation."

Here are a few legislative tools that were developed by Legal Services lobbyists and that Phillips found during his brief tenure as OEO's chief:

● "How to Pass Legislation" was prepared by an employee of OEO's Pine Tree Legal Assistance Project in Maine and tells all about gaining "public support" for legislation as well as about "lobbying and hearings."

● "Substantive Legal Areas" is a package of memorandums from "backup centers detailing specific matters in their respective areas of expertise where legislative action might be appropriate."

● Terry Hatter, executive director of the OEO-funded Western Center on Law and Poverty of Sacramento, California, is quoted as saying, "It is highly important that the poverty lawyers who achieved the court victory also have input into the legislative changes it has necessitated."

● In "Tactics for Legislative Negotiations," the Milwaukee Legal Services Program also made its lobbying activities crystal clear.

● Legal Services director Fred Speaker in 1971 told an annual meet-

---

*According to reports on file with the Clerk of the House.

ing of the tax-subsidized National Legal Aid and Defender Association: "I am convinced that the reform of established law through litigation and legislative advocacy must be a primary priority of the Legal Services program."

There are many good things that government can do to protect and promote the welfare of its citizens, particularly the poor. Legal Services—at least on the federal level—is not one of them. The program has been rife with abuse and has become in effect a virtual tax-paid program to fund legislative advocacy by representatives of a political minority.

Perhaps a case can be made for this on the state level, specifically in states where the need is great enough. But $190 million isn't even going to begin to provide legal assistance to the millions of Americans the federal government has categorized as poor. Meanwhile, the millions more who do not fall within that category and who find it equally difficult to afford legal assistance are provided with nothing from this program but the cost. It is a program that has become a vehicle for political and legislative crusaders while the taxpayers—including the poor—have footed the bill.

31

Office of Consumer Affairs

$1.5 Million

WHAT COULD BE MORE IN THE INTEREST OF consumers than saving them $1.5 million in taxes? That's what I would propose by abolishing this HEW agency, which was set up in 1971 to advise the President on everything and anything concerning consumer affairs.

The federal government is loaded with agencies that look out for the consumer and, one hopes, his best interests. These agencies include the Food and Drug Administration and its numerous bureaus, the Consumer Product Safety Commission, and the Federal Trade Commission, to name only a few. Like everything else in government, the cost of the Office of Consumer Affairs is going up. It got by with $1.2 million in fiscal 1974 and asked for $1.4 million in fiscal 1975.

Why an agency needs this much money just to advise the President is anybody's guess. Virginia H. Knauer, its director under the Nixon administration, was noted for going around the country making speeches in behalf of consumer causes. Late in 1974 she announced the beginning of a weekly radio program, at government expense, to provide consumers with tips on how to cope with inflation. Her office also issues literature and periodic reports on consumer topics. The office, however, does little if anything that is not duplicated elsewhere. In fact, consumers would owe Mrs. Knauer a debt of gratitude if she announced that her office was being dismantled in an effort to cut down on government spending and thus aid in the fight to curb inflation. Meanwhile, if the President isn't being advised by other, far bigger consumer-related agencies within the government, he should be.

32

Export-Import Bank

$518 Million

THERE ARE NUMEROUS GOVERNMENT PROGRAMS that work in direct competition with and to the detriment of the American worker and taxpayer, but few quite so deceptively and despairingly as the Export-Import Bank.

Stripped of all its rhetorical sleight-of-hand defenses, this agency removes billions of dollars from the U.S. capital-starved market and turns it over to foreign governments and investors at tax-subsidized, bargain-basement interest rates. Thus, the American business-man—already taxed to the hilt—finds he must compete with foreign businesses that purchase their machines and goods from the U.S. with cut-rate seven percent Export-Import loans while he must finance his equipment and commodities at almost twice that rate in the private capital market. Obviously, under these antifree market rules, it's hard to stay in the game.

The *Wall Street Journal* said there was no way anyone "could persuade us that wresting capital away from Americans, then forcing it abroad through the subsidy mechanism, does anything but distort relative prices, misallocate resources and diminish revenues, with zero effect, at best, on the trade balance."

The chief arguments put forth by the bank's supporters is simply this: By loaning low-interest money to foreign investors to purchase U.S. manufactured goods and equipment, they are providing increased jobs for Americans. However, everytime the Ex-Im Bank helps foreign competition to produce goods or services—for which the American businessman must in fact pay far more to produce—it is selling American jobs.

The Ex-Im Bank was established as a relatively modest program in 1945 but today has a multi-billion-dollar lending authority. Congress extended the agency's lending authority in 1974 for four more years at a $25 billion level. In the 1974 fiscal year Ex-Im took $1.1 billion out of the capital market and in 1975 was expected to borrow more than $1.2 billion from it. Congress, in 1971, passed legislation removing the bank's borrowing transactions from the federal budget to make the deficit look smaller. Nonetheless, its transactions still result in the same fiscal deficit effect and constitute a continuing drain on the private money market—hurting taxpayers, business, and workers alike.

Pan American Airways a couple of years ago had to issue bonds through the Chemical Bank of New York—at an 11⅛ percent interest rate—to buy some jumbo 747 airplanes. Meanwhile, foreign airlines in competition with Pan American could buy the same 747s with Ex-Im Bank money at six percent (its lending rate at the time). Charles Tillinghast, Jr., chairman of TWA, said his airline, like Pan American, was losing money flying the North Atlantic route against foreign competitors who purchase Boeing 747s and other U.S. manufactured aircraft with subsidized Ex-Im loans. Tillinghast said that if TWA could obtain loans at the Ex-Im's low rate, the airline would save $11 million a year in finance charges. Nearly one-third of all Ex-Im Bank's direct loans go to finance the purchase of American aircraft by foreign airlines or their governments at the bargain discount of $7 million to $20 million per aircraft below the price paid by American carriers.

The idea behind the Ex-Im Bank is to encourage the purchase of U.S. products. Yet this is ludicrous reasoning when applied to the aircraft industry since almost all commercial aircraft purchased by foreign compet-

116

itors come from the United States. Without the Ex-Im Bank, foreign investors would still buy aircraft from the only country that makes most commercial aircraft—the United States. So the bank's existence is worthless on this score. But it encourages purchases of other U.S. exports, its defenders say. However, one devastating fact destroys even this argument: 96 percent of all U.S. exports are made without Ex-Im Bank direct loan assistance.

"We are interested in sales, that is right," remarked Ohio's Democratic Congressman Wayne Hays, "but I am not interested in the export sale of American aircraft in order to put American airlines out of business."

By making such loans at interest rates far below what American businesses can borrow, the United States is in effect exporting American capital, thus making money more scarce and, therefore, driving up interest rates.

The Nixon administration through the bank granted a $180-million loan at six percent to the Soviet Union to help finance a large fertilizer-producing complex there. Meanwhile, by giving credit to the Russians at half the rate charged domestically, we support the industrial base of the Communists while the U.S. experiences its own fertilizer shortages and U.S. fertilizer producers receive little or no help from their own government. This of course is only one of many loans made to the Soviets. One of the largest truck plants in the world is the Russian Kama River plant built with $342.1 million in American money. John Dent, Democratic congressman from Pennsylvania, complained that the bank helped the Soviets purchase 260 circular knitting machines costing $5.6 million.

"What are we talking about?" Dent asked one day on the floor of the House. "Do we need someone over in Russia using these machines to compete with our workers so they can send their products all over the world?"

Another Democratic representative, Charles Vanik of Ohio, charged: "We have severe shortages in a number of industries—such as the energy and fertilizer industries—yet we are making subsidized loans to the Soviet Union to improve their energy and fertilizer-production capabilities." In fact, much of the loan authority increase sought by the bank was planned for investments in the Soviet Union, Congressman Vanik said. Major loans were being considered for development of energy resources under the Soviet's so-called North Star project in Siberia, estimated to cost between $7 and $8 billion. Meantime, as our own energy needs become more critical every day, it is proposed that subsidized U.S. capital be sent abroad to develop energy resources for the Soviet Union.

Incredibly, despite strong House sentiment expressed in a vote of 319-80 on December 11, 1973, opposing loans and credits to the Russians due to their restrictive emigration policies, the bank went ahead and approved over $100 million in loans and guarantees to the Soviets.

A *Pittsburgh Press* editorial on May 26, 1974, said it best: "It may be news to the White House, but it isn't to U.S. intelligence agencies, that the Soviet Union can well afford to pay cash or to arrange for normal commercial credits for what it wants to buy in this country.

"Russia is a major exporter of oil and oil products to hard-currency areas.

"It will get a windfall profit of $1.5 billion to $2 billion in 1974 from the fourfold boost in crude prices imposed by the Arab oil cartel. . . .

"Only this month the Soviet Union gave Argentina $600 million in credits for a vast electric power project.

"Can anyone explain why Russia should get a $180 million loan from the United States when Russia can afford to lend Argentina $600 million?

"By granting credit to the Soviet Union at half the rate charged domestically and to many friendly countries, the U.S. taxpayer is subsidizing and giving foreign aid to the Kremlin's industrial base."

It may be true that bank loans help create some additional American jobs, as its defenders argue, but it should also be obvious that six or seven percent loans would create jobs anywhere—even in the United States! And without boosting foreign competition. The bank's supporters say it earns a profit for taxpayers of about $120 million a year but in fact loan reschedulings and delinquent loan payments are substantial, rising to over $250 million in delinquent payments and over $350 million in rescheduled payments from fiscal 1969 through the end of 1973.

Its supporters stubbornly deny that the bank's borrowings amount to a subsidy but their effect can be deemed nothing but taxpayer subsidies.

In its "Special Analysis of the Budget," the Office of Management and the Budget concluded: "Even when totally outside the federal budget, such as the Export-Import Bank, and without support from budget resources, federal guarantees and other means of federal credit aid have a significant economic impact and social cost. They alter market mechanisms in determining who gets scarce credit resources, in what order of priority, and at what cost. As a result the structure of the economy is altered, capital markets are affected in major respects, and fiscal policy objectives are made more difficult to attain.

"The net budget impact of interest concessions made to borrowers on direct loans for any single year includes the subsidy costs arising from both new loans and outstanding loans made in previous years. By the same token, all new loan commitments at submarket interest rates will add to budget outlays for all future years during which the loan remains outstanding. Once newly subsidized loans are committed, the future costs are largely predetermined and the net subsidy cost becomes relatively uncontrollable."

According to OMB, the subsidy of the Ex-Im Bank at the old six percent rate amounted to $2 million for every $100 million in commitments. This of course is now lower since the bank increased its rate to seven percent. OMB figured that the present value at 9.5 percent discount of future subsidies committed under bank loans would come to $518 million for fiscal year 1975.

The General Accounting Office, Congress's auditing and investigating agency, agreed with OMB that significant subsidies are involved in the Ex-Im Bank's loans.

For example, the GAO said in a 1971 report: "The interest and other financial expense reported by Ex-Im Bank include interest charges on a significant part of the borrowings from the U.S. Treasury at rates lower than the rate prevailing at the time the funds were borrowed. Had the Treasury charged Ex-Im Bank interest rates approximating the full cost of the funds, the bank's interest and other financial expense would have been increased by about $11.9 and $16.9 million in fiscal years 1971 and 1970, respectively, and the net income from operations for the years then ended would have been correspondingly reduced."

Democratic Senator Lloyd Bentsen of Texas once proposed amending the Ex-Im Bank's authority to prevent it from financing "those exports involving the finances of foreign industrial capacity whenever the production resulting from that capacity would significantly displace like or directly competitive production by U.S. manufacturers."

Senator Bentsen is on the right track but doesn't go far enough. Helping foreign countries build steel plants and textile mills and other industries only serves to help America's competition and does further

119

injury to our balance of trade. The Export-Import Bank should be phased out of existence.

The Russians might be a little upset by such an occurrence because they've been on the Ex-Im Bank's gravy train, but—as the *Wall Street Journal* pointed out—they and other foreign investors would eventually adjust by getting into the private capital markets.

Congressman H. R. Gross said it so well: "It is long past time when this government starts putting the American consumer, the American taxpayer and the American businessman ahead of the citizens and governments of almost every other nation on earth."

33

International Development Association

$1.5 Billion

HOW WOULD YOU LIKE TO BORROW $1.5 billion from the United States government and have 50 years to pay it back interest-free, with a 10-year grace period to boot?

Incredible as it may sound, these are the terms under which the World Bank's International Development Association (IDA) has distributed billions of dollars to its 66 member countries. The fund from which IDA doles out its largess is raised by 25 nations and of course by far the biggest contributor is good old Uncle Sam—up until 1974 providing almost 40 percent of the fund's billions.

The 1974 authorization for America's commitment to give an additional $1.5 billion spreads the contribution out over four annual installments of $375 million each from 1976 through 1979. (The U.S. has already contributed over $2 billion to the fund.) The House on January 23, 1974, resoundingly rejected the IDA authorization by a vote of 248 to 155 but then reversed its action six months later after Wright Patman of Texas, chairman of the House Banking and Currency Committee, sweetened the bill with a provision allowing Americans to own gold. That was enough to bring the necessary number of conservatives around to supporting the entire measure. Congressman Steven Symms, Republican from Idaho, walked onto the floor during the IDA debate and announced to House members, "I just came from the cloakroom, where I made a phone call to my broker. I asked him what the price of gold was today. He said, 'It is $1.5 billion. I understand it is for sale today down at the Capitol.' "

The stated purposes of IDA are "to promote economic development, increase productivity and thus raise standards of living in the less-developed areas of the world. . . ." Through mid-1973 IDA had authorized a total of 428 development credits amounting to $5.8 billion. Its loans are for 50 years and bear no interest. After a 10-year grace period, one percent of the principal is repayable annually for 10 years and three percent in each of the remaining 30 years. There is a yearly service charge of three-quarters of one percent on the disbursed portion of each loan to cover administrative costs.

Defenders of America's participation in the fund will tell you that it goes for projects in countries where the per capita yearly income is less than $375. But the issue here is not whether all of this money from American taxpayers is being spent for humanitarian needs—some of it is, a lot of it isn't—but whether we can afford it. I maintain that we can't.

And canceling this program would not exactly turn Uncle Sam into Uncle Scrooge. Over the past 27 years the U.S.A. has committed over $266 billion in foreign aid to countries throughout the world. We have foreign aid programs coming out of our ears. We have given and we have given generously. But eventually we will come to a point where we must say, "Enough is enough."

"What has disillusioned most of us is the fact that the money has not gone to these poor people," complained Democratic Congressman Clarence Long of Maryland. And indeed there have been abuses.

For example, it is no secret that many of the recipient countries take the funds and lend them out again to other countries at the prevailing interest rates. Moreover, at least 30 percent or more of IDA's loans have gone for industrial power plants and transportation and a far smaller percentage for agriculture to feed the hungry and education to teach the illiterate. India, for example, consumes 35 percent of IDA's budget annually and has received about $2.5 billion in loans since IDA's inception in 1961. But it is evident that these vast resources helped give India the financial wherewithal to develop its nuclear bomb.

IDA gave $20 million to Bangladesh only to have the money used for a telecommunications program, which included development of microwave, UHF, and VHF systems. Meanwhile, Bangladesh has been ravished by famine. Similar expenditures of dubious benefit to the truly poor have been made with IDA's easy-credit loans.

Often, one wonders if our generosity is even appreciated. Seldom is it reciprocated. In 1973 the U. S. loaned the Sudan $11 million for agricultural development, gave it $2.2 million in grants for refugee assistance, and a $2.1-million long-term, low-interest loan to purchase 20,000 tons of U. S. wheat. In addition, we have loaned Sudan $60.5 million. But when the U. S. ambassador to the Sudan was assassinated there by Palestinian terrorists, what did this recipient of U. S. dollars do? The assassins were freed and sent back to the Palestine Liberation Organization.

But more to the point is whether a nation that has showered hundreds of billions of dollars around the world on nations both rich and poor can continue to do so under our present economic circumstances. How in all rationality can we continue borrowing money at up to eight or nine percent interest and lend it out to other countries without interest?

The hard-pressed American taxpayer will be called upon to pay for this $1.5-billion gift through bonds or Treasury notes. Put in its harshest perspective, this $1.5-billion authorization will come out of taxpayers' pockets at the rate of $1 million a day over four years, not to mention the interest that Americans—not IDA recipients—will pay to borrow this sum.

Earlier in the 1974 legislative year Congress approved an emergency foreign aid package that provided $150 million to several Asian, African, and South American countries struck by disasters. The need was obvious and the United States responded with compassion and a sense of urgency. Such humanitarian assistance—when needed—should be provided as deserving situations arise. But at a time when America is plunged into debt, raked by inflation, and plagued by a trade deficit, IDA's no-interest giveaway program is no longer affordable.

Again the House's fiscal watchdog, H. R. Gross, summed it up when he admonished his colleagues thus: "Mr. Speaker, it is shameful that this bill was ever brought before us in the first place. It should be rejected out of hand and by such a one-sided vote that the entire world will know that the generosity of the American people—unsurpassed in recorded history—has been stretched, and cruelly stretched, to the breaking point."

34

White House Office
of Telecommunications
Policy

$8.4 Million

THERE ARE TWO OFFICES OF TELECOMMUNI-
cations within the government, spending more than $9.6 million an-
nually. Only one of them is necessary.

Within the White House's executive offices there is the Office of
Telecommunications Policy (OTP). Its overall function is executive
agency supervision of all national communications. Within the Commerce Department there is the Office of Telecommunications. Its
primary function is to provide the analysis, engineering, and technical
services to support OTP. It is a strange, dual arrangement that was born
during the first term of the Nixon administration: the two offices exist
physically apart even though they are working essentially on the same
tasks.

OTP and its sister agency within Commerce were set up under an administration reorganization plan in 1970 whose goal was to bring every
facet of the federal government under effective White House

policymaking control. Much to the consternation of the Federal Communications Commission and a number of other agencies concerned with similar communications functions within the government, OTP and its then-director Clay T. Whitehead proceeded to do just that.

Whitehead assembled a staff of 55 people within the executive offices, worked his budget up to $8.4 million as of fiscal 1975, and ranged over the waterfront of communications—from criticism of network news programs to policy questions concerning a multiplicity of communications operations both inside and outside government.

The question, however, is whether this new bureaucracy within the White House was necessary in the first place. Talking to OTP officials is an exercise in communications gobbledygook. They will lead you to believe that the work of OTP is absolutely vital; that OTP is breaking new ground in communications research; that OTP and only OTP can handle the communications work it has assigned to itself. But upon closer examination one finds that the bulk of its inflated budget is really funneled through Commerce's Office of Telecommunications (which has a $1.2-million budget of its own) to conduct reams of research and study programs. Who did these studies before the appearance of OTP? I asked one official. "Nobody," he said. "These studies weren't even being done before us."

Many of OTP's inquiries are of low priority. Others are not. Some research programs probably are the proper responsibility of the Federal Communications Commission, the National Science Foundation, and other agencies, including the Office of Telecommunications. The primary nonresearch task handled by OTP—the authority to assign communications frequencies within the federal government—was previously handled by the Office of Emergency Preparedness. This task could be returned to that office. Meantime, OTP should be dismantled according to an evaluation of which policymaking and research responsibilities should be discontinued and which should be transferred to other appropriate agencies.

35

Council on
Environmental Quality

36

Office of
Environmental Quality

$2.5 Million

ESTABLISHMENT OF SPECIAL OFFICES AND councils under the White House to provide the President with independent policy guidance is a trend begun under previous administrations and used excessively under the Nixon administration.

It seemed for a while that for every major department or agency of government there was to be a special council of independent advisers in the White House. The Council on Environmental Quality is one of them, and like a number of other special offices it duplicates some of the work and endeavors of its parent agency—the Environmental Protection Agency (EPA).

The council consists of three members appointed by the President with the advice and consent of the Senate. The Office of Environmental Quality provides the staff for the council, which is supposed to develop and recommend to the President national policies to promote environmental quality. EPA and other environmental programs were budgeted to over $1.1 billion during the 1975 fiscal year. These resources are more than enough to analyze any changes or trends in the national environment and to propose necessary policy recommendations to the President. Thus, the Council on Environmental Quality should be merged into EPA's well-financed machinery. The $2.5 million saved would be like a breath of fresh air.

37

Joint Brazil-
United States
Defense Commission

38

Joint Mexican-
United States
Defense Commission

THESE COMMISSIONS HAVE TWO THINGS IN common: both were established in 1942 and both are run by a single top military official supplied by the Joint Chiefs of Staff.

The taxpayer cost of his salary and that of one assistant and a secretary to run both commissions is minimal and by the officer's own admission he spends little time working on them*—his primary job being the U.S. delegation to the Inter-American Defense Board (discussed in the following chapter). Still, at a time when military spending is under constant attack, the two commissions are anachronisms that should have been retired years ago. Both are an outgrowth of our World War II relationships to Mexico and Brazil, the only Southern Hemisphere neighbors to send forces into the war.

The Joint Brazil-U.S. Defense Commission is composed of military

---

* It is difficult to calculate exactly how much time is spent on them, thus no cost-savings is given.

delegates from the two countries and was created by agreement between the two governments in May 1942 for the purpose of making bilateral studies of problems concerning defense of the Western Hemisphere.

The Joint Mexican-U.S. Defense Commission was established in February 1942 by the Presidents of the two countries to study common defense problems. "What do they do?" I asked a Defense Department spokesman, noting that they possessed staffs, offices, telephone listings, and were carried as viable agencies in the *U.S. Government Organization Manual*. "Oh, they've been inactive for I guess the past 15 years," he said. "They haven't been a going entity for some time now."

"Don't they have any function to perform?" I asked incredulously. His reply couldn't have been any more candid: "Oh, socially, perhaps."

We maintain strong diplomatic ties with both countries and any military liaison activities could be handled through the military attachés of each embassy. There appears to be absolutely no compelling reason why these two commissions should continue to exist. By now their studies, if not their socializing, should be finished.

39

Inter-American Defense Board

$1.8 Million

THE *U.S. GOVERNMENT ORGANIZATION MANUAL* is filled with agencies with names like this one, and even when you talk with the military attachés who usually staff their offices you come away with a feeling that you still don't know what in the world they do.

The Inter-American Defense Board receives its funding through the Organization of American States, which obtains 66 percent of its funds from the United States. The OAS allocated $2.8 million for the board's 1974-76 budget, thus $1.8 million would be the U.S. share of this board's cost.

The board was founded on March 30, 1942, with the onset of World War II, to defend the Western Hemisphere against the Axis powers. The purpose of the board is to study and recommend to its Inter-American members measures for closer military cooperation and preparation against aggression. Also included in its program is the Inter-American Defense College at Fort McNair in Washington, D.C., which provides top-level military officers of member nations with the opportunity for advanced studies in social, political, economic, and military problems. In other words, the board is one more expense item we could just as well do without.

40

Consumer Information Center

$886,000

THIS PROGRAM, UNDER THE GENERAL SERV-
ices Administration, is supposed to encourage federal agencies to develop and release relevant consumer information and to help make the
public aware of such information. Anyone who knows anything about
the swollen public relations offices of government agencies must wonder
what encouragement they would need.

GSA publishes, thrice yearly, a free "Consumer Product Information
Index" listing more than 200 selected federal publications of interest to
consumers. Consumer information is also distributed through the media
under this program. In fiscal 1974 the center sought $221,000 over its
1974 funding, so business must be booming. Meanwhile, dozens of
agencies are producing and distributing millions of pieces of consumer-
related literature. The Government Printing Office shelves are filled
with it. Everything from how to tile your bathroom to how to buy a step-
ladder. Let's let the existing agencies handle their own public information programs and let the consumers pocket $886,000.

41

National Institute of Education

$70 Million

THE FEDERAL GOVERNMENT POURS BILLIONS OF dollars into aid to education every year and every year we hear that the same old problems, such as inadequate schools and poor reading achievement, remain. In many cases, they've grown worse. At the same time, HEW is also spending hundreds of millions of dollars to research a vast range of subjects, apparently in search of a better way to educate America's youth. Much of this spending is at best of marginal importance. Much of it is flagrantly wasteful. While it is becoming increasingly apparent that basic educational skills such as reading, writing, and arithmetic are being insufficiently emphasized in our schools, the government is spending a fortune in tax dollars on dozens of rather esoteric-sounding studies that delve into the very sociological and cultural underpinnings of society. The Office of Education is filled with such wasteful research but one agency within it, the National Institute of Education (NIE), perhaps best illustrates how the government's education dollar is being shamelessly squandered.

Here are a few examples gleaned from the institute's fiscal 1974 funding program list:

- Study of How Children Form Peer Groups: $ 29,000
- Identifying Individual Learning Differences in Infants and Toddlers: $103,000
- Study of Infants' Ability to Control Their World in Home and Non-Home Situations: $ 75,000
- Speech Patterns of Teachers as They Affect Childrens' Language Development: $ 49,000
- A Study of the Goals Laymen Expect of Secondary Education: $258,000
- Policy Studies Examining the Relationship Between Family and School: $ 34,000
- A Follow-up Study of the Employment Status of Students Who Graduated from High School in 1960: $350,000
- A Study of How Schools Respond to Their Clientele: $173,000
- A Study of the Influence of Childrens' Environment on Their Speech Patterns: $ 46,000
- A Study of Sex Role Learning and Sex Discrimination: $300,000
- Study of Sex-Bias and Sex-Fairness in Guidance Materials: $ 50,000
- A Study of the Career Decision Making Process: $150,000

By September 1974 the institute had spent over $200 million in its two and a half years of operations. It seemed to be sailing along nicely—putting in a fiscal 1975 budget request of $130 million, up from a 1974 budget of $75.5 million—until the Senate Appropriations Committee took a long look at its research programs and decided that it had had enough.

"The Institute's success in nearly all endeavors it undertook can be considered minimal, at best," the committee said in its report. "Many favor the dismantling of NIE and a return of research activities to their appropriate bureaus in the Office of Education. This may well be the wisest possible course of action."

The Senate panel was strongly critical of NIE's disinclination to eliminate "marginal, less-productive educational research and development projects. Efforts should have been concentrated on more goal-oriented activities, rather than on a proliferation of research projects covering a much too broad spectrum."

Some of NIE's projects appear to have merit, particularly those dealing with handicapped and disadvantaged children. But the vast majority of them are of little immediate, or even long-range, benefit to improving the education of our children. Dozens of studies appear to have no value whatsoever and, in the words of the committee, are "extrinsic to the real needs of our nation's education system." Many of them, concerned with curriculum development and other areas, only duplicate studies and program development being undertaken by the states under other federal education grants.

Although the Senate Appropriations Committee recommended no money for NIE for fiscal 1975, the House agreed to give the institute $80 million for the year, with the compromise figure of $70 million agreed to in a House-Senate conference. The Senate's anger over the wastefulness of this program is fully justified. NIE should be abolished.

42

Council on Legal Educational Opportunity

$750,000

THE COUNCIL ON LEGAL EDUCATIONAL Opportunity (CLEO) was set up to provide scholarships so that more people could become lawyers. This at a time when the Labor Department says we have almost twice as many law school graduates than we need.

The aim of the CLEO scholarship program is to help "persons from disadvantaged backgrounds to undertake training for the legal profession." It was begun under the OEO's Office of Legal Services and authorizes HEW grants "to provide nonprofit organizations representative of legal education and the legal profession for the purpose of (1) selecting and counseling such persons; (2) paying stipends to such persons and in such amounts as the commissioner may determine to be appropriate; and (3) paying for any administrative expenses."

The program flies in the face of some overwhelming statistics. A record number of law school graduates passed the bar examinations in 1974—30,075—whereas only 16,500 legal jobs are expected to be available each year. There are numerous professions in America that are in seriously short supply. The legal profession is not one of them.

The House passed legislation modifying the program in June 1974 by a lopsided vote of 310-53. Before the bill's passage, there was this exchange between H. R. Gross and James O'Hara (D.-Mich.), who championed the program:

> Gross: *Mr. Speaker, I am curious about this program of taking care of so-called disadvantaged persons with respect to a law degree. . . . Why not doctors?*
> O'Hara: *I do not know. There is no reason why not doctors, I would suppose. But I know of no such program.*
> Gross: *Of course, there ought to be some answers as to why this is limited to the legal profession. Are we short lawyers in this country?*
> O'Hara: *I do not believe there is a great undersupply of lawyers.*
> Gross: *Is it not the fact that many young men are unable to get into law schools this year because they are full?*
> O'Hara: *Yes, it certainly is.*
> Gross: *Why did the gentlemen pick out lawyers? . . . Is it not the fact that we are probably in shorter supply of blacksmiths than we are of lawyers in this country, people who can shoe horses and do general blacksmithing?*

Chesterfield Smith, a past president of the American Bar Association, has estimated that by 1985 there will be twice as many lawyers as there are today. Smith expressed doubt that "the present American legal system can profitably employ them all," but added hopefully that "a changed system which would enable anyone who needs a lawyer to afford to hire one, would create a need for even more lawyers." There can be little question that what Smith had in mind was a much expanded Legal Services Corporation that would provide tax-subsidized lawyers throughout the country on a scale yet undreamed of by its present supporters.

There are many professions that desperately need manpower nowadays. Doctors and nurses come immediately to mind. The government provides hundreds of millions of dollars to help young people obtain an education in any field of their choosing. The student assistance

137

provisions in the 1975 education funding bill as passed by the Senate included $685 million for basic grants to 1.1 million students, $300 million for college work-study assistance, $240 million for supplemental grants to exceptionally needy students, and $286 million for direct loans to more than 682,000 students. By June 30, 1975, total student loans from the government were expected to reach an estimated $8.1 billion.

Beyond all this, it is reasonable to expect that the federal government will not specifically seek in its student aid programs to boost a particular profession that is already overloaded, further crowding law schools that have all the students they can handle. There are many avenues of assistance open to anyone who wants to go to college, is qualified, and does not have the funds needed to pay the rising costs of higher education. The Guaranteed Student Loan Program and the National Direct Student Loan Program are two of those avenues. Under the latter, loans may be partially forgiven if the student goes into certain areas of education where teachers are needed. This is a sensible approach to fulfilling a need where one is evident. The need for more lawyers—and this program—is not evident.

43

U.S. Botanic Garden's Congressional Florist Service

$64,000

ON ANY GIVEN DAY ON CAPITOL HILL YOU MAY see a man pushing a plant- and flower-laden flat cart down one of the corridors of the House or Senate office buildings. The lush ferns and palms and the bright carnations it carries are regularly supplied to senators and congressmen to decorate their offices. As they die, wilt, or are taken by members and staff employees to their homes, the Botanic Garden gladly replaces them and the taxpayer picks up the bill.

The U.S. Botanic Garden's enormous greenhouse is located at the foot of Capitol Hill. Its interior is an oasis of dense vegetation and quiet pools surrounded by a wide variety of palms, cycads, ferns, cacti, orchids, fruit trees, and other tropical and subtropical plants. It is one of the finest botanical collections in the world and is offered as an educational facility for students, botanists, and floriculturists to study rare and interesting specimens.

The Botanic Garden has for years made its plants available to members of Congress as a "free" service. In 1973 its nearly $1-million budget greened congressional offices with between 12,000 and 14,000 plants, more than double what it provided in 1970.

Members of Congress receive a wide range of benefits, including the best health insurance and pension plans in the world. They are provided with gymnasiums with swimming pools, saunas, massage tables, and a variety of other exercise and rest facilities. There is no need to add free plants to their long list of benefits, particularly since there is widespread evidence that many plants are finding their way into the homes of members of Congress and their employees.

A Scripps-Howard reporter who probed the purloined-plant scandal quoted one congressional aide as saying, "Everybody does this." The news report noted that while Botanic Garden records showed there should have been 15 plants in the office of Rep. David N. Henderson (D.-N.C.), his office's "greenery was spare." One aide sheepishly said, "To be perfectly honest with you I suppose we abuse this." Some aides said plants were taken home because they needed repotting or were wilting, even though the Garden takes care of all its plants and makes "house calls." "Someone took one home to make it get some sunlight," an aide to Rep. Clarence Long (D.-Md.) said. "But they're going to bring it right back." The report found similar excuses concerning missing plants in other offices. One member, according to "reliable sources," had a summer intern drive some fresh plants to his home in Tennessee. Others described the practice as "well known" and "systematic" in many offices. "It is a ripoff," one aide said.

Many Americans would like to have beautiful plants regularly supplied to them and periodically replaced with freshly potted ones or have their drooping philodendrons cared for by their personal horticulturists. A look at the prices charged for plants nowadays by nurseries and florists shows why many taxpayers can't afford such luxuries. While members of Congress are beating their breasts over inflation and calling on Americans to make sacrifices to help hold down the cost of living, it seems only fair to ask these same congressmen to make similar sacrifices. Here's one expense that's ripe for congressional sacrifice. The greenery should go.

44

Federal Impact Aid
to Education
(B Category)

$354.6 Million

WHEN CONGRESS ENACTED A SPECIAL AID TO education program in 1950 for federally impacted areas, it made some sense. When a major military installation existed in an area, the school districts found they were burdened with the additional costs of educating the children of families living on that installation. The local government couldn't tax the military base as it could a business or industry, and the military personnel who lived on the base were beyond the reach of local property taxes and thus made no contribution to the tax needs of the school district. The result was an increase in the area's schoolchildren without a commensurate increase in tax revenues to support the additional costs to school them. What resulted was often poorly financed and inferior schools.

Congress sought to alleviate this problem through the enactment of the Impact Aid Program. The idea was that school districts burdened with the added costs of educating children of federally connected personnel would receive additional aid over and above their regular federal grants. However, over the past 24 years this program has been amended and expanded to the point where it is no longer limited to aid to schools serving children of parents who live on federal property. Instead, it has been funneling increasingly large amounts of federal aid to school districts irrespective of any actual burden imposed by a federal presence. President Nixon said in 1970 that 70 percent of the federal impact payments to schools were "for children of federal employees who live off base and pay local property taxes."

In fact, Duane J. Mattheis, a top U.S. Office of Education official, declared in a June 12, 1974, article in the *San Diego Union:* "Literally hundreds of the eligible districts (under the aid program) . . . suffer no appreciable adverse effect on the ability to support schools due to the presence of federally-connected children. On the contrary, a federal activity is often a major and much-prized economic benefit. Only a small percentage of districts receiving impact aid actually suffer a heavy federal impact, as in the case of school districts serving a military base."

According to U.S. Office of Education statistics, some 4,700 school districts qualified for impact aid to education in 1973, covering 2.2 million federally connected children. But of this total, only 367,000 were regarded as "A category" children whose parents lived and worked on tax-exempt federal installations.

The statistics further showed that over 1.8 million "federally connected" children fell within the aid program's "B category," children whose parents lived in private homes liable to local property taxes. Under the "B category" program, local school districts were also compensated for the federal impact of the children and it is this program that should be terminated.

The best illustration of the tax revenues that are being wasted under this program is the $6.2 million in aid going to one of the wealthiest areas in the country, Montgomery County, Maryland. The funds are provided because of the so-called federally caused financial burden brought on the county's schools by the families of federal workers in nearby Washington, D.C. and the surrounding area. About $6.1 million of the $6.2 million in impact aid is given to the county under "B category," while most of the parents of the 28,000 "B category" students work outside the county, most of them in Washington. Almost all of them live in private residences whose property taxes go to support the county's school system. "Here is a county," Mattheis said, "which can and does provide excellent education from its own resources, receiving large payments for its federally-connected students, when their parents already pay sufficient local residential property and income taxes to support the schools at a level well above the national or state average."

There no longer is any sensible need for this program. Federal installations, which are sought after by many communities, pour considerable revenue into affected areas and thereby raise their entire economy, often making them among the nation's most affluent. As a result, further school aid is going to relatively wealthy communities while poorer communities remain in obviously greater need of assistance. President Nixon, in a message to Congress calling for reform of the program, said, "Nearly twice as much federal money goes into the nation's wealthiest county through this program as goes into the one hundred poorest counties combined." Congress has begun a snails-pace effort to try to phase this program out over several years, but its supporters manage to win higher funding for it every year.

Abolishing the wasted revenues in this program does not mean that aid to legitimate impacted areas cannot and should not continue under a new program of tightened eligibility requirements that eliminates aid to school districts where the federal impact is small or nonexistent. Obviously, if impact aid to wealthier districts is reduced or terminated, it could mean more funds would be available for school districts having the greatest need, based on a strict formula that weighs the true federal impact upon an area's economy and its schools.

45

Government Travel Costs

$481.6 Million

THE GOVERNMENT IS SPENDING ALMOST $2 billion a year on travel by federal employees. Despite presidential exhortations for government departments and agencies to conserve energy, out-of-town travel at the taxpayer's expense is thriving. Much of it is unneeded and wasteful. The government spends a fortune for telephone Wats lines—which provide unlimited long-distance calls for a basic monthly charge—and employees could do more communicating by phone instead of jetting about the country and the world on the public tab.

The government spent $1,926,615,000 in the 1975 fiscal year for travel. It had racked up more than $1.8 billion and $1.7 billion respectively in the two previous years. A simple 25 percent across-the-board reduction in government travel would result in a saving of more than $481.6 million, not to mention a fortune in energy costs.

144

Although we hear a great deal about congressional junkets, often a wasteful expenditure of public funds, the fact remains that nearly 99 percent of government travel is engaged in by the executive branch. The legislative and judicial branches account for the remaining one percent.

William V. Roth, Republican senator from Delaware, has studied this subject closely and observes that "inflation and the need to conserve energy have caused millions of Americans to cut back or cancel their travel plans. Virtually every business and private organization has been forced to reduce its travel budget to save money and fuel. Yet the federal government has increased its travel budget by nearly $100 million in the past year. With inflation being fed by excessive federal spending, and with the vital need to conserve energy, there is absolutely no justification for the federal government to spend such sums on travel expenses.

"While a certain amount of travel is necessary in the ordinary course of business, reductions in travel could be achieved by using the telephone, teletype and other modern means of communications. . . . There's nothing wrong with writing a letter either."

Roth, who introduced a bill calling on President Ford to reduce federal travel expenditures by 25 percent, examined the travel budgets of a number of government agencies and found that the bureaucracy has literally taken the nation's travel promotion slogan "See America First" to heart. He found, for example, that the Department of Health, Education and Welfare would spend a total of $77.9 million in fiscal 1975 on travel and transportation alone, $5 million more than would be spent by the Department of Transportation on its own transportation expenses.

Roth also found the Social Security Administration planned to spend over $21.6 million on travel, while the Department of Agriculture's transportation budget exceeded $112 million. In sharp contrast to Agriculture, the State Department, with embassies, missions, and offices around the world, budgeted only $28 million for travel. The National Science Foundation set its travel budget at more than $1.9 million. And the Selective Service System, which is being kept needlessly alive on a standby basis, budgeted $1 million for travel expenses (can you imagine how much it would spend if asked to administer a draft?).

These are just a handful of examples of the degree to which almost every department, office, agency, commission, board, or council flies around the country and the world for God knows what reason. Even the smallest government entities find some rationale—by hook or by crook—for out-of-town trips. A little-known agency such as the National Capital Planning Commission, created to plan the development of the nation's capital, budgeted $18,000 for travel. Very often when agencies plan major meetings or regional and national conferences, they will be held in some of the swankiest resort capitals of the country, or the world. One conference held by the National Endowment's Expansion Arts Advisory Panel was in San Juan, Puerto Rico, a delightful place to hold a meeting but not necessarily when it's at the taxpayer's expense.

In December 1973 Congress approved a Roth resolution that called on the government to cut back its energy consumption by one-third. Roth said that it resulted in energy savings between January and April 1974 of some $240 million, or the equivalent of 30 million barrels of oil. The government is constantly calling upon Americans to make sacrifices whenever a crisis looms. Here is one area where the government can begin practicing a little self-sacrificing of its own and at the same time save taxpayers close to half a billion dollars. Perhaps we should replace the slogan "Conserve Energy" with "Conserve Tax Dollars."

46

Highway Beautification Programs

$26 Million

REMOVING UGLY BILLBOARDS AND JUNKYARDS
and otherwise improving the scenery along our nation's highways should
be a top environmental priority, but not for the federal government.
General highway beautification programs are responsibilities that quite
properly belong to local governments.

Like everything else, however, this is an area in which Washington
has become involved. Yet, at a time when other more costly federal programs deserve higher priority, not to mention the obvious necessity to
control spending, this is one program that can and should be phased out
of existence.

The highway beautification program is administered in the Department of Transportation under the Federal Highway Administration. The
program funnels federal funds to the states to help pay the costs of con-
trolling outdoor advertising, eliminating junkyards, and landscaping
lands along highways with trees, shrubs, and grass. Funds are also
provided to develop scenic overlooks, clearings, and roadside rest

areas. Plantings along highways also help to prevent erosion.

Most of the money being obligated to the states goes for billboard control. For example, of a total $145 million authorized by Congress for fiscal years 1970 through 1973, $99.5 million was for billboard control, $14 million for cleaning up junkyards, and $31.5 million for highway landscaping. Now, removal of unsightly billboards that scar the countryside is certainly a worthy endeavor, but it can by no means be deemed a high priority for America. In fact, Congress approved legislation in 1965 to provide these general funds for highway beautification because the highway trust funds available for this purpose were being spent by the states on other highway-building expenses.

In fiscal 1974 Congress appropriated $30 million to be paid out to the states for highway beautification contract obligations incurred under its authorization. In fiscal 1975 the appropriation was $26 million. I have used the $26-million figure as the amount that would have been saved in fiscal 1975 if the program had been summarily abolished by Congress or at least deferred. Authority for the program was to expire June 30, 1975. If the program was totally terminated, Congress would probably want all of the approved state expenditures paid by the Federal Highway Administration. However, had Congress decided in fiscal 1975 not to approve any funds for that year (because of the government's severe deficit) and promptly ended the program—contracts or no contracts—it would have saved federal taxpayers the remaining outlays. Not only that, it would have saved the $1 million in administrative expenses it costs to run the program annually.

Some so-called congressional budget-cutters beat their breasts over "priorities" and agonize over the budget being all but uncontrollable. And in the case of the highway beautification program, much of the authorized money is already in the spending pipeline and it remains for Congress to make good on its promises. And perhaps it should. But no further authorizations should be approved. In a time of massive budget deficits, the program sticks out like—well, like an ugly billboard.

47

Department of Agriculture's Economic Research Service

$21.7 Million

THE AGRICULTURE DEPARTMENT PROVIDES AN enormous amount of data, research, and analysis for the farmer and the agricultural industry as a whole through its Economic Research Service (ERS). Departmental spokesmen say ERS is absolutely essential to the survival of American agriculture. But a closer look at some of the reports it is turning out at the taxpayer's expense indicates that perhaps ERS is not all that vital as one might think. Consider the following:

In July 1974 ERS issued a $113,417 study titled "Mothers' Attitudes Toward Cotton and Other Fibers in Children's Lightweight Clothing." The 113-page report was the result of interviews with 2,161 mothers from coast to coast. After boiling down a mass of statistics, it concluded that mothers prefer—get ready—children's clothing that requires no ironing. The study developed such amazing findings as: "Most mothers interviewed said their daughters wear dresses in warm weather, but more often wear dungarees, slacks, and shorts. The preferred fiber for these garments, as well as for tops and blouses, is a blend of cotton and polyester, primarily because it requires no ironing." The report continued, "Mothers of boys reported a preference for dungarees, sport shirts, and slacks made of a blend of cotton and polyester because it requires little or no ironing, is long lasting, and is neat looking." The cost of this study figured out to $52.40 per interview.

The report was issued by the ERS through its Food Consumption Demand Analysis and Consumer Interest Program. The head of the program, Dr. Alden Manchester, seemed genuinely apologetic about the study during an interview but insisted that "they [his program's other studies] aren't all that bad." A look at some of his office's recent publications seems not fully to bear that out. Many of his agency's reports appear to ignore the question, "Why are our tax dollars being spent on this?" Here's a sampling:

● "Homemakers' Preferences, Uses, and Buying Practices for Selected Noncitrus Fruit and Fruit Products, a Preliminary Summary Report"

● "Men's Attitudes Toward Cotton and Other Fibers in Selected Clothing Items"

● "Consumers' Buying Practices, Uses, and Preferences for Fibers in Retail Piece Goods"

● "Consumers' Preferences for Fresh Tomatoes" (Doesn't everybody prefer them?)

● "Consumers' Preferences, Uses, and Buying Practices for Selected Vegetables"

Many studies like these are being undertaken by ERS, which employs 502 economists among a total staff force of about one thousand people. Dr. Manchester's program alone was budgeted for $859,000 in fiscal 1975, a small portion of $21.7 million ERS spent to produce hundreds of studies and publications, many of which are of dubious value to the farmer—for whom, after all, the Agriculture Department was created. Many of ERS's marketing reports, however, are clearly for the sole benefit of specific food and fiber industries, which would no doubt pay to produce such reports for themselves if they were not being prepared for them at the taxpayer's expense. An examination of 564 reports issued by ERS between 1972 and 1973 shows that many of these studies were prepared for, or at least presented to, various industry associations that dealt in the very market commodity being analyzed by the report.

For example, a report titled "An Economic View of Soybeans and Food Fats in the 1980s" was presented before the Institute of Shortening and Edible Oils, Inc., while a study titled "Economic Outlook for Edible Vegetable Oils in the U.S." was presented before the Potato Chip Institute. A study entitled "Outlook for the Dairy Industry" was prepared for the annual convention of National Milk Producers, while a paper titled "U.S. Exports of Raw Wool and Wool Tops: Recent Trends and Market Implications" was presented to a meeting of the International Wool Textile Organization in Rome.

Dr. Manchester, in fact, told me that many of the studies produced by ERS were specifically designed to help various trade and processing groups "to find out what they [consumers] want from their products. We get calls from them [industry representatives] all the time," he said, "asking us, 'When are you going to get that study out?' " Obviously a number of industries benefit from these reports, which they receive free while the taxpayer pays the cost.

Criticism of the Economic Research Service and its work does not necessarily mean that all the reports it issues are worthless. On the contrary, a number of ERS reports, particularly its periodically issued "situation-outlook" reports (there are 22 of them) and long-range marketing forecasts, are important and useful to the Agriculture Department's work and to American and world agriculture generally. Much of the information ERS uses in its supply and price analysis reports comes from the Statistical Reporting Service (SRS), the survey-making arm of the Department of Agriculture. The SRS issues, among other things, regular reports on crop and livestock production. Such data-gathering is essential to understanding the ebb and flow of America's agricultural resources. But many of the studies being done by its research counterpart, ERS, raise serious questions about whether taxpayers are getting their moneys' worth from this agency of government. Here's a broad sampling of what ERS has been churning out:

• "Implications of Population Trends for Quality of Life"

• "Quantitative Dimensions of Decline and Stability Among Rural Communities"

• "Potential Supply and Replacement of Rural and Urban Males of Working Age 20 to 64 for States and Other Areas of the United States, 1970-80 and 1960-70 Decades"

- "Percent Nonwhite and Rural Disparity in Nonmetropolitan Cities in the South"
- "Changing Retail Activity in Wisconsin Villages: 1939-1954-1970"
- "Age Stratification and Value Orientations"
- "Age Stratification and Life Attitudes"
- "A Look at the Dairy Farm Labor Image"
- "Discussion of Social Attitudes, Economic Growth, and Place of Residence"
- "Socioeconomic Trends and Nonfarm Demands for Resources in the Tennessee Valley"
- "Economic Analysis of the Campground Market in the Northeast"
- "Need for Research on Land Policy Issues Associated with Strip Mining"
- "Alternatives to the Property Tax for Educational Finance"
- "Mobile Home Residents in New Hampshire"
- "Spice Trends in the United States"
- "The Changing Pattern of Eating Out"
- "A List of References for the History of Agriculture in the Midwest, 1840-1900"
- "A List of References for the History of the Farmers' Alliance and the Populist Party"
- "Books on Agricultural History Published in 1970"
- "On-Farm Peanut Drying Justified"
- "Potential for Oilseed Sunflowers in the U.S."
- "If You're a Cattleman, How Do You Compare with This 'Profile'?"
- "Teletype Auctioning: Valuable to Canadians, Still Virtually Untried in United States"
- "Computer Decision-Making Seen as Aid to Baking"
- "Cut Flower Imports: The Impact on the American Market and the Tri-State Area"
- "Changing Patterns in the U.S. Carnation Industry"
- "Demand and Cost Consideration Affecting Oilseed Processing in South Vietnam"
- "The Market for Food Consumed Away from Home: Dollar Value Statistics"
- "Demand for Farm Raised Channel Catfish in Supermarkets: Analysis of a Selected Market"

- "Rural Zoning in the United States. Analysis of Enabling Legislation"
- "Who Owns America's Land? Problems in Preserving the Rural Landscape"
- "Outdoor Recreation Resources in the Chicago Metropolitan Area"
- "Spain—A Thriving Commercial Customer"

The question that immediately comes to mind is what do many of these studies have to do with growing more food for America and helping the farmer? It is highly questionable whether these and similar research and analytical reports are in any way promoting the well-being of American agriculture, which, after all, should be the paramount responsibility of the Economic Research Service. According to one ERS official, "Industry collects a lot of statistics about itself and we get a lot of statistics from industry." If that is so, the agribusiness giants and the various commodity and trade industries could provide much of this material for themselves (or at the very least pay the government for the cost of producing it).

"If the Economic Research Service were disbanded tomorrow, what would happen to American agriculture?" I asked an ERS administrator. "Probably nothing," he replied, adding that in the absence of an ERS the nation's agricultural industries would move in to provide most of the data research and marketing analysis necessary to compete in the world's food and fiber markets. Additional demand for research analysis and marketing statistics would no doubt be met by the private sector, which has evidenced a rise in independent marketing and economic study firms throughout the country. "They would continue to have farm economists in private industry who would perform the analysis and forecast functions we are now doing," this ERS official said.

Despite a lengthy annual list of ERS reports, it is worth noting that with all their data and surveys, the Agriculture Department was caught with its pants down when the Soviet Union surprised the world with its $1-billion purchase of U.S. wheat and other grains in 1972 and virtually took the American farmer to the cleaners. Instead of informing the farmer of the impending purchases, which resulted in driving up grain prices, the Agriculture Department confessed that it too was surprised by the grain deal. Thus, the farmers sold their grain short and lost a fortune. It almost happened again in the fall of 1974 but President Ford called in the nation's major grain firms and Soviet plans to purchase 3.4 million tons of grain were stymied (although the Soviets eventually purchased 2.2 million tons).

As emphasized earlier, there are certain ERS situation-outlook reports concerning foreign agricultural trade, commodity supplies and forecasts, and other analyses that are undoubtedly necessary and should continue, perhaps under the aegis of the data-gathering Statistical Reporting Service, which has a budget of almost $30 million. Some staff carryover from ERS would no doubt be necessary but nowhere near the 1,000 employees it is presently carrying. A long interview with a top Agriculture Department budget official resulted in one startling admission concerning ERS's value. The gentleman (who wished not to be identified by name) conceded, after much questioning and discussion about what was vital in ERS and what was not, that ERS could put out its regularly issued reports—though little else—for half its $21.7-million budget. "Yes, we could handle the current situation reports on a budget of $11 million, sure," he said (though he believed the "level of quality" might suffer). I happen to think that 22 situation-outlook reports could be issued for a lot less than $11 million, but it's noteworthy that a top departmental official believes ERS's basic work—stripped of its other studies and reports—could be performed for less than half the present budget. This official also went on to state that two major divisions in ERS, the Economic Development Division and the Natural Resources Division, could be abolished totally without significantly affecting the department's work or the performance of the nation's agriculture. These two divisions alone have annual budgets totaling over $3.8 million.

Clearly, an examination of the bulk of ERS's output shows that much of its work is at best of marginal importance and should be mothballed. America's wealthy and powerful agricultural business community certainly has the financial resources to provide much of the marketing analysis and forecasting now being provided "free" by the American taxpayer. The Department of Agriculture is now costing taxpayers about $9.2 billion a year (two-thirds of it is for food welfare programs). Certainly, within that goliath of a budget there should be funds enough to provide whatever statistical and analytical resources are needed to meet our farm program needs without wasteful studies that ask mothers what they prefer in children's clothing.

48

The Pentagon's "Top Brass" Dining Rooms

$1.9 Million

THERE ARE RESTAURANTS IN WASHINGTON where you can lunch on an appetizer (choice of soup or juice), a broiled red snapper, three vegetables, a salad, and baked Alaska, all for $1.75. Or would you prefer the "deluxe" luncheon with filet mignon or lobster for $2.50? How can they do it at that price in these days of inflation? you ask. The answer is that the cost of running these restaurants is picked up by the taxpayers at about $1 million a year. But don't bother trying to make reservations, because their clientele is restricted to top military brass only. The restaurants, you see, are in the Pentagon.

The "restaurants" consist of five private dining rooms cloistered inside the Pentagon in which some 400 admirals, generals, and other top-ranking civilian Defense Department officials elegantly lunch each day on entrees prepared and served in crisp military tradition by 86 enlisted men.

Each dining room costs the government an estimated $200,000 a year to operate. Prices on the menus range from $1.75 to $2.50. Within this range are complete lunches—including sirloin steak, broiled red snapper, rock lobster tail with drawn butter, and grilled filet mignon—plus everything else from soup to nuts. The bargain-basement prices are supposed to cover the cost of the food, Pentagon officials say, but they do not cover the salaries of the enlisted cooks and waiters or other overhead expenses such as utilities and use of the restaurant space. These are paid for with your tax dollars. One civilian cafeteria operator in the Pentagon said that labor costs in most cafeterias add 50 percent to the cost of food prices, and that doesn't include the cost of utilities and other expenses.

Pentagon panjandrums maintain that the restaurants are the only place where military brass can conduct business lunches "in a secure environment." They further argue that the executive dining rooms are a necessary "fringe benefit" that helps to encourage generals and admirals to stay in the military. Interestingly enough, while the Pentagon's chiefs dine in luxury on a more than adequate menu, the Defense Department has been suggesting that it may be necessary to economize on the enlisted men's menu in order to cut costs. The Defense Department spends around $2 billion a year to feed some two million military persons. Meanwhile, in the Gold Room of the Pentagon blue-jacketed Filipino stewards recruited by the Navy wait upon our military leaders. They are also employed in dining rooms operated by the Joint Chiefs of Staff and the Navy. The Air Force and the Army prefer to use their own enlisted men in their private dining rooms. Use of the dining facilities is restricted to admirals and three-star generals and their immediate deputies, and civilian Defense Department officials at the assistant-secretary level and their chief deputies.

The House Appropriations Committee has been sharply critical of the subsidies needed to feed our top-paid officers in the manner to which they have become accustomed. The committee said in a 1973 report that the amount being spent on the five Pentagon dining rooms and 18 other private military messes in Washington and throughout the world* was "excessive and the amount of the subsidy should be substantially

---

* There are, in addition to the five Pentagon dining rooms, six other private military messes located in and around the Washington area.

reduced. There does not appear to be any reason why some of the Executive Dining Rooms operated in the Pentagon cannot be consolidated for use by the various services rather than each service having its own facilities.

"When compared with the subsidies paid by other government agencies for this purpose, the amount used by the Department of Defense is substantially greater."

But the aristocratic practice continues as it has for years, without any sign from the military brass that they are prepared to tighten their real belts and "condescend" to eat in the four cafeterias or the eight snack bars used by some 25,000 other Pentagon employees—though the food is admittedly worse and more expensive. In two dining rooms, which the cafeterias run with waitress service, the cheapest luncheon available was a club sandwich with cole slaw for $1.70, and prices went up to $2.30 for a pot roast dinner. Until the Army dining room boosted its prices up to $1.75, you could get a soup-to-nuts meal that included sirloin of beef en brochette teriyaki for $1.00.

With the nation's military budget under increasing attack, it wouldn't be a bad idea for our top brass to demonstrate that they are willing to lead in a total cost-cutting effort throughout the Defense Department. Defense Department figures indicate that the 23 private mess facilities are costing taxpayers almost $2 million a year. Here's a specific area where the military could slash that cost from its budget by simply abolishing the private dining rooms and eating with the other lower-ranked military personnel in the regularly provided mess facilities and cafeterias. It would no doubt boost the morale of civilian and military personnel alike to see their superiors eating alongside them instead of in restricted "country club" dining rooms. UPI Pentagon reporter Warren Nelson wrote in one news dispatch that "many Pentagonians who aren't entitled to eat at the elite messes in the building ask why generals, who make $31,000 to $51,000 a year, should get the special savings." One worker remarked, "I thought food stamps were for the poor."

Abolishing the special-privilege dining rooms with their cut-rate prices and fancy menus would certainly be a dramatic gesture to the public that the military is sincerely trying to cut down on military costs without sacrificing the defense of our nation. The dining rooms should be closed down.

49

Foreign Aid

$2.7 Billion*

THERE IS AN ALMOST ENDLESS STRING OF reasons why we should end America's foreign aid program as it presently exists. But of all the reasons I've either heard or read, none is more compelling than the simple declaration that the United States cannot afford to develop, feed, house, and arm the entire world.

"Charity begins at home" is a cliché that immediately came to mind when President Ford went before Congress in October 1974 to call on the American people to cough up an additional $2.6 billion through a five percent income tax surcharge to provide public jobs for the unemployed, increased unemployment compensation, and a tax cut to spur business expansion. Meanwhile, Ford was also fighting for a foreign aid authorization bill that originally sought $3.2 billion to hand out around the world. The Senate and House had chopped the request by almost a billion dollars. Still, the reduced $2.7 billion in economic and military

---

* This foreign aid cut is based solely on the aid authorization measure approved by Congress for fiscal 1975. At the time this book was written Congress had not approved an appropriations bill. On March 24, 1975, after months of delay, Congress passed a $3.6 billion appropriations measure to fund the program through June 30, 1975.

aid the administration proposed giving away was pretty close to the surcharge amount Ford wanted taxpayers to shell out in additional tribute. No one, unfortunately, suggested that, instead of seeking to burden an additional tax on middle-income Americans, the President could temporarily defer part of our foreign aid program in the midst of an uncontrolled inflation-recession crisis and use that money to help boost the economy. Such an idea, apparently, was unthinkable.

Foreign aid has to be one of the most enormously extravagant spending programs ever undertaken by Uncle Sam. It has grown by leaps and bounds, each year pouring billions upon billions of tax dollars into almost every country on the face of the earth. It has become an annual spending binge to which the United States seems to have become permanently addicted, shoveling millions into countries both large and small, rich and poor, some of which most Americans never even knew existed. Strangely, no one seems to ask, "What are we getting out of all of this?"

No one really knows precisely what the United States spends totally in all its foreign assistance programs each year—though the best figures place the entire annual expenditures at almost $11 billion. The U.S. budget is filled cover to cover with foreign aid and loan programs of one kind or another, many of which are virtually hidden. A number of them operate with individual authorizations and appropriations all their own, such as the Export-Import Bank. There are also the International Development Association, the Asian Development Bank, and the Inter-American Bank, among others. Finding other foreign aid programs in the budget can at times be like looking for the proverbial needle in a haystack. For example, there was foreign aid money, $5 million in fiscal 1974, in the Federal Highway Administration budget to help build the inter-American highway through Panama and Colombia. There was also more than half a billion dollars in the Agriculture Department budget for Food for Peace, not to mention the Defense Department's separate military assistance program. Robert S. Strother, writing in *Reader's Digest*, noted: "Numerous aid expenses weren't identified anywhere in the budget—for example, U.S. defense equipment, mainly Navy vessels, loaned at no charge to foreign countries. American fishing vessels off its coast with patrol boats which were, in some cases, provided by U.S. military-assistance programs. U.S. taxpayers have had to reimburse shipowners for more than $5 million in 'fines' paid to Ecuador.

"It would take an army of accountants to comb through the federal budget and total up all aid."*

The $2.7-billion fiscal 1975 foreign aid authorization program I have chosen to add to my list represents only the "tip" of America's foreign aid iceberg. But this Foreign Assistance Act of 1974 also represents what is essentially the backbone of the U.S. aid program. Abolish it, or at the very least sharply cut it back, and the way will be open to reform America's entire aid program.

Liberals and conservatives have for years been widely split over foreign aid. Liberals, to a large degree, have focused their criticism, and their spending-cut amendments, on military aid. Conservatives have primarily been critical of economic aid. I would significantly reduce both.

In its report on the authorization aid bill, the Senate Foreign Relations Committee proposed that the U.S. "provide grant military aid to foreign countries not as a habit, but rather only in specific instances where such assistance is clearly warranted. At present, the far-flung network of U.S. military assistance advisory groups, military missions, and military groups gives bureaucratic momentum to the perpetuation of an extensive program the rationale for which each year has become increasingly dubious. Through this bureaucracy, the U.S. continues—almost habitually—to dispense hundreds of millions of dollars of weapons in pursuit of such vaguely defined goals as 'stability,' 'balance,' and the 'maintenance of friendly relations.' "

Suspicious as I've always been of the liberal Foreign Relations Committee, their approach—if carried out prudently—would save America billions and probably deny military aid to countries that would be better off without it, and perhaps force other countries to buy more of their arms from us (which wouldn't be bad for our balance of payments).

The committee found that the military aid program "not only escalates the destructive potential of international conflict but also enhances the relative power of the military within those societies and thereby creates undesirable tendencies away from the very democratic processes which the program, in its origins, was intended to defend."

Perusing the list of countries to which we provide military aid is an

---

* "Foreign Aid: What Does It Really Cost?" September 1974.

exercise in outrage, at least in most instances. Why are we giving these nations, year after year, millions upon millions of dollars in weaponry? For example*: $11.3 million in arms aid to Ethiopia, $2 million to Tunisia, $70,000 to Ghana, $100,000 to Liberia, $860,000 to Morocco, $300,000 to Zaire, $3.3 million to Bolivia, $1.6 million to Uruguay, $1.1 million to El Salvador, $1.1 million to Honduras, $1.3 million to the Dominican Republic, $1.3 million to Guatemala, $1.4 million to Paraguay, $800,000 to Peru, $700,000 to Argentina, $700,000 to oil-rich Venezuela, $25,000 to Senegal, $50,000 to the Sudan, $50,000 to Mali, $24,000 to Austria, $80 million to Turkey, $15,000 to Sri Lanka, $220,000 to Saudi Arabia, $35,000 to Nepal, $94.2 million to Jordan, $100,000 to India, and $200,000 to Afghanistan. U.S. military aid to many of these and other countries simply defies understanding. Such arms aid has become, as the committee stated, a "near-addictive habit," in part fed by an overseas network of U.S. military missions established to oversee and administer America's weaponry treasure.**

As expected, the bulk of our 1975 military and economic aid was slated for Indochina: $1.2 billion for South Vietnam alone, $377 million for Cambodia, and $70 million for Laos. (Massive assistance was also provided for Israel, with about $639 million in economic and military assistance contained in the fiscal '75 authorization bill. We have poured billions of dollars and thousands of American lives into South Vietnam and the argument that the U.S. cannot now let it fall to Communist North Vietnam is a strong and convincing one. Still, our aid there must be sensibly controlled by an evenhanded assessment that provides South Vietnam with the means to defend itself against a Communist takeover, tempered with stringent guidelines to reduce the millions that are now wasted through graft and corruption.

But if the partial list of nations receiving annual arms assistance from the United States gives vent to taxpayer anger, the list of more than 100 countries slated to receive a grand total of $8.4 billion in overall eco-

---

* All of these figures represent what the administration proposed spending on military assistance in these and 22 other countries in fiscal 1975.

** There are 43 U.S. military missions located around the world. The Defense Department estimated that in fiscal 1975 they cost over $74.4 million to operate, $16.8 million of which was in foreign military assistance funds, with the remainder, $57.5 million, in defense appropriations.

nomic and military assistance and arms credit sales in fiscal 1975 is even more staggering to behold. Here are some choice selections—and hold onto your wallet: Algeria, $1.4 million; Botswana, $1.7 million; Cameroon, $1.3 million; Ethiopia, $47.9 million; Ghana, $15.6 million; Kenya, $8.9 million; Liberia, $9.6 million; Morocco, $49.1 million; Sierra Leone, $2.5 million; Sudan, $15.9 million; Tanzania, $12 million; Togo, $2 million; Tunisia, $21.3 million; Upper Volta, $2.2 million; Zaire, $15.2 million; Afghanistan, $17.1 million; Fiji, $606,000; India, $113,894; Korea, $416 million; Nepal, almost $7 million; Oman, $181,000; Philippines, $103.7 million; oil-drenched Saudi Arabia, $220,000; Ceylon, $18.8 million; Thailand, $88.5 million; Tonga, $333,000; Turkey, $232.4 million; South Vietnam, almost $2.4 billion; Brazil, $69 million; Chile, $84.9 million; Colombia, $52.8 million; Jamaica, $11.4 million; Egypt, $253.1 million; Malta, $9.5 million; Spain, $4.6 million.

The figures are depressing, not necessarily because of the individual sums and their size but because of the wasteful way in which the U.S. tries to spread its wealth across the face of the earth, touching the tiniest of islands and nations as if we could buy away all the problems of the world. We can't.

The United States' worldwide aid program should be scrapped. In its place there should be a select list of countries representing only those in dire need of military or economic help. Certainly, South Vietnam, which is fighting for its very independence, would qualify, as would Israel and a small number of others. The same approach should be taken for any and all economic assistance. We daily read of millions of people starving in some God-forsaken drought-stricken land such as West Africa's Sahel region, Bangladesh, or elsewhere. Yet we continue to read in our newspapers of Congress approving billions of dollars each year in foreign aid that, unfortunately, is scattered too thinly and too loosely to provide effective, efficient, and lasting relief to the people who truly hunger and thirst and have no shelter or clothing or medical care. I am thinking primarily of countries in crisis—whose problems can only be defined as emergencies.

Foreign aid should not be like an annual life insurance policy for every nation on earth in which the U.S. continues year after year to pay the premiums, regardless of the policyholder's financial condition. There is not enough money in our Treasury—even if it were totally turned over to foreign assistance—to support the undernourished peoples of the world.

What the United States can do is to use its vast resources more sparingly but in a far more concentrated fashion. Instead of thinly spreading $11 billion around the circumference of the earth, couldn't we better concentrate, say, $6 billion on the severest cases of hunger, disaster, disease, or whatever need exists in the world in any given year? U.S. foreign aid, it is clear, has been spread far too thinly, making it in many cases ineffective and squanderous. We have poured billions of tax dollars into India, for example, in military and economic assistance ($8.8 billion between 1946 and 1973 in various loans and grants), only to see that nation use its resources to invade Pakistan and develop and explode a nuclear bomb. And still we witness the continuation of hunger and misery there on a scale so vast that it has numbed us into thinking that India will always be a country of starving and dying people.

Consider this dispatch in the fall of 1974 by a *London Observer* reporter from Cooch Behar, India: "There is rice in the markets, within sight of people dying of hunger, but they cannot afford to buy. In the ex-princely state of Cooch Behar, now a district with 1.5 million people, more than 1,000 have starved to death in the last two months. . . . People have become so weak that hundreds more are now dying every day in the four districts of Cooch Behar, Bangkura, Purlia, and Jalpaiguri. The government of India has been trying to play down the extent of the famine both at home and abroad, but even a casual visitor can see it for himself. Everywhere there are people, especially small children and old people, so emaciated that they could scarcely survive, even if substantial relief were expected in the coming weeks. But no relief is in sight, and next month, when cold weather is added to hunger, the death toll in this state will climb. The immediate cause of the famine—the worst since the Bengal famine of 1943—is not outright lack of food, but that the poor have no money to buy it. The West Bengal government has no funds for more than token relief, while the central government in New Delhi has not yet accorded the situation any special priority." (They're too busy making nuclear bombs, no doubt.) The reporter, Walter Schwarz, went on to observe that some of the starving received a daily plate of gruel, which cannot even be digested by starving children or adults, but only those holding cards issued by village authorities "can get even this. Those without cards are forcibly turned away, and leave, moaning or weeping, to die."

If India has the millions to develop a nuclear bomb, it has the money to help feed many of its starving people. Clearly, the starving are not of high enough priority for the Indian government. In any event, the situation in the West Bengal region is obviously an emergency, one in which a totally reformed U.S. aid program could act quickly and resourcefully to deal with. Certainly, a reading of the list of U.S. aid makes it clear that billions of dollars in assistance are going to countries where there is no widespread famine, no starving children, no natural disaster. When the need in these countries is compared with the severe drought conditions in the Sahel, the earthquake disaster in Nicaragua, and the famine in India, obviously annual U.S. aid payments are not required; indeed, in several respects, many of these countries are doing quite well for themselves.

America's aid program must be radically changed and only Congress can change it. Past administrations have sadly been propagandists for continuing more of the same. Presidents are vulnerable to the difficulties of maintaining foreign policies, sensitive to the pleas and pressures of foreign ministers and the need to continue "good relations" with each and every foreign government. Congress, on the other hand, is not as susceptible to these kinds of pressures. Only Congress can put an end to our uncontrolled addiction to foreign aid. On that point, Professor Thomas Shelling of Harvard testified before the Foreign Relations Committee:

"It is always difficult to terminate aid programs, military or other. There is always an apparent shock or trauma when the United States seems to be severing a long-standing connection with a country, when it seems to be stopping its appreciation of the country as a recipient of aid. I think it is often the case, too, that countries receiving aid can intensify and exaggerate the pain and the anguish and the poverty that go with the cessation of an aid program. The Congress is often in a very strong position to make aid termination look less discriminatory. The Congress can often take steps that are recognized by recipient countries as applying rather more universally than the bilateral diplomatic negotiations that the countries have with the Executive Branch. Countries can always hope to importune the Executive Branch to continue something, especially something that does not cost a great deal of money, and for the Executive Branch to refuse is very often construed by the country as

164

lack of appreciation by the Executive Branch.

"If the hands of the Executive Branch are sometimes tied, if the Executive Branch is not available to that kind of importuning, very often the pain and the shock of the termination of a program to which a country has become accustomed turn out to be very small and, particularly, the country's government will take its own steps to reduce rather than to enhance the likely diplomatic shock of such termination."

A study released in May 1974 by the Agency for International Development reviewed all American foreign aid from 1945 through June 30, 1973, and found that the United States gave a net total of $163.7 billion in that period. Other studies have placed the true total cost of all economic and military foreign aid expenditures in this same period from over $300 billion to over $477 billion, depending upon whether you figure in the total interest paid on the money America has had to borrow to give away.

Nobody has any real idea what America is spending totally each year on all foreign assistance programs. Until Congress can restructure its appropriation measures so as to place foreign aid under a single umbrella, instead of scattering it across dozens of different programs and agencies, there is no way it can be effectively cut back totally. But the mainline foreign aid authorization bill would be a good place to start showing we mean business about ending rampant, worldwide foreign assistance and get down to the business of using what little Uncle Sam can really afford to help the world's truly unfortunate.

50

Smithsonian Institution's Scientific and Cultural Research (Special Foreign Currency) Program

$2 Million

THERE'S A PICTURE FOREVER EMBEDDED IN my mind of a mother in India holding her naked child, his bony, listless body all but emaciated. I envision that picture and the children starving to death in India when I think of the $6,000 budgeted for that country, under the Smithsonian Institution's scientific and cultural research programs, for an "Anatomical and Ecological Study of the Indian Whistling Duck." How many children in India would that $6,000 have fed? Or how about $70,000 for the study of wild boars in Pakistan. Or $2,000 for an examination of the "Comparative Population Dynamics of Competitively Exclusive Lizard Species" in Yugoslavia. Or $11,540 for "A Biochemical Investigation of *Rana esculenta*, a Bisexual Frog of Possible Hybrid Origin" in Poland. Rest easy, little children ... the ducks in India and the lizards in Yugoslavia must come first.

There are many research and study projects like these that are financed each year under the Smithsonian's auspices. In fiscal 1974 it spent $4.5 million on them. Congress, reacting to intense criticism of this program, slashed the Smithsonian's request for an additional $4.5-million appropriation to a flat $2 million for fiscal 1975.* Since 1966 the Smithsonian has been receiving annual appropriations of foreign currencies that are held by the United States in various countries and that the Treasury Department determines are in "excess of the normal needs of the United States." The Smithsonian is just one of nine federal agencies that receive these excess foreign currencies. Without any doubt, however, the Smithsonian's use of these excess currencies is the most wasteful. Briefly, here is how "excess" foreign currencies work:

Under the provisions of the Agricultural Trade Development Assistance Act of 1954 as amended (better known as Public Law 480) and other measures, the United States has sold surplus agricultural commodities and materials to other countries. The U.S. accepted payment for the food and materials in foreign currencies, rather than in dollars (this of course was at a time when the U.S. balance of payments was favorable). In other words, the acceptance of foreign currency allowed food to flow to famine-stricken countries that had not enough convertible currency to acquire urgently needed foodstuffs. Under the sales agreements made between the U.S. and each food-purchasing country, the currencies were to be spent by the U.S. in that country. The funds were established usually in the purchasing nation's central bank and disbursed by the U.S. embassy under instructions from the various federal agencies entitled to use those funds in their programs. The money was also used for the construction and operation of our embassies in the affected countries as well as for loans to American businesses, and various research and education programs, supposedly of benefit to the U.S.

The provision in Public Law 480 allowing current expenditures for research and study to continue states that U.S.-owned foreign currencies should be made available to U.S. government agencies to "collect, collate, translate, abstract, and disseminate scientific and technological information and conduct research and support scientific activities overseas including programs and projects of scientific cooperation be-

---

* The sum was actually reduced to an effective $1 million for its research programs, with the other $1 million earmarked specifically for a United Nations program to salvage the temples of Philae in Egypt.

tween the United States and other countries such as coordinated research against diseases common to all of mankind or unique to individual regions of the globe, and promote and support programs of medical and scientific research, cultural and educational development, family planning, health, nutrition, and sanitation." Many of these goals sound valid and worthy enough but the truth is that much of this excess foreign currency—which could be used for immediate and serious problems to feed and provide health care for the poor, for example—is being wasted on very low priority programs in what are some of the poorest countries in the world.

The Agriculture Department's Agricultural Research Service (ARS) spent the equivalent of about $61.2 million in foreign currencies from 1961 through 1973. ARS's active grants totaled about $34.8 million in early 1974. Where does the money go? In Yugoslavia the U.S. spent $36,078 in 1972 on "An investigation of the effect of fermentation processes on the quality, taste, and aroma of Oriental tobacco, to obtain information for use in improving the quality of American cigarettes" (while the U.S. Surgeon General is warning Americans that cigarette smoking is hazardous to your health). In Pakistan the ARS spent $27,112 on "Investigations on the natural enemies of marijuana . . . and opium poppy." In Poland it spent $69,111 on a five-year study on "the long-term storage of acorns."

The Smithsonian maintains that "most" of its activities supported by foreign currencies "can be considered building blocks in the complex structure of science which continues to advance mankind's welfare." Its use of the funds supports research in four general areas: archaeology and related disciplines; systematic and environmental biology; astrophysics and earth sciences; and museum programs. "Most of the major advances in man's understanding of his world," the Institution said in a release on its foreign currency program, "have been achieved by a process of accumulation of small correct conclusions by many scholars which have eventually provided the basis for major revisions in our thinking." Maybe so, but no moderate man can examine the work being performed under these studies—knowing the serious condition of both the world and our own Treasury—and not conclude that the funds are being poorly and even wastefully expended.

Here's a representative sampling of the kind of research the Smithsonian has been undertaking the past several years with these funds:

168

- "A Review of the Recovery Data Obtained by the Bombay Natural History Society's Bird Migration Project"
- "Ecogeographic Analysis of a Climate Map of Ceylon with Particular Reference to Vegetation"
- "Further Investigation of Glass Factories in Western Galilee"
- "The Skeletal Biology of Human Remains from Sites in the Lake Kainji Area of Nigeria"
- "The Ivory Horse Bits of Homer and the Bone Horse Bits of Reality"
- "Studying Skulls in Egypt"
- "The Excavation of Two Glass Factory Sites in Western Israel"
- "Parallel Evolution of Shell Characters in Succineids Inhabiting Waterfalls"
- "A Red Sea Grouper Caught on the Mediterranean Coast of Israel"
- "First Report of the Yale-Bombay Natural History Society Studies of Wild Ungulates at the Gir Forest, Gujarat, India"
- "Cytological Studies of Pacific Land Snails"
- "Fishes Collected During a Midwater Trawling Survey of the Gulf of Elat and the Red Sea"
- "Revised List of the Mediterranean Fishes of Israel"
- "On the Stability of an Encounterless Self-Gravitating Constant Density System"
- "Semen of the Ceylon Elephant"
- "Two Red Sea Fishes in the Eastern Mediterranean"
- "Vermeulenia—a New Genus of Orchids"
- "Pharmacy in Medieval Islam and the History of Drug Addiction"
- "Recovery of a Spotbill Duck in U.S.S.R."
- "Sponges of Red Sea Origin on the Mediterranean Coast of Israel"

Now, it is argued by those who support this kind of spending that the titles are usually highly misleading and that if each project is examined in its entirety, its scientific worth and potential benefit to man's knowledge of his world will be obvious. Not in the programs I examined. Consider the one about India's Whistling Duck. The study was conducted through Texas Tech University in conjunction with the Bombay Natural History Society. A project explanation said the studies "on the life cycle of whistling ducks in this country, as compared to anatomically nearly identical ducks in India, suggest that the Indian ducks have developed the ability to adapt to a more varied environment. Discovery of the reasons why a nearly identical bird species has different abilities to adapt may suggest ways in which an endangered species can be introduced and preserved in a different environment."

Fine, and perhaps environmentally important. But in India the world is confronting far different problems as well. How do we justify spending $6,000 on a duck study when millions of human beings need food? But we have to get rid of this excess currency some way, the program's supporters counter. One way or another it has to be spent, they say. Okay, but why not on building health clinics, emergency food distribution facilities, or food-producing programs?

Here's the official explanation on the study of Poland's bisexual frogs: "Opinion has differed for some time as to whether *Rana esculenta* is a hybrid or a separate species of frog. This study, in cooperation with the Zoological Institute in Poznan, will not only attempt to classify properly this frog by enzyme and protein analysis, but will provide the opportunity for Polish and American scientists to share the latest techniques in species identification." No doubt a worthy scientific endeavor but not, certainly, a top priority for government spending. It just does not meet the strict criteria of need that must be applied to all federal research programs.

James Davidson, the scourge of government waste and the executive director of the National Taxpayers Union, told *Wall Street Journal* reporter Arlen J. Large that these specific examples of waste were "not as important as the whole effect. People just aren't prepared to put their minds around some multi-billion-dollar program like the space shuttle, which may be more preposterous than a $10,000 study of clams. The issue I'm trying to raise is not that some specific little item should be cut out of the budget, but to make people conscious that money is being wasted. Then if they put enough pressure on Congress, the members may be more in the mood to cut something as big as the space shuttle."

Davidson stressed that he wasn't attacking the scientific value of many of these projects, "but just pointing out to people that this is the kind of spending that provides very little benefit to you." Large pointed out that some agencies also using the foreign currencies, such as the National Science Foundation and the National Institute of Health, try to keep their study project titles as murky as possible to avoid critical media and congressional attention. "You avoid anything that sounds off base," Large quoted an NIH official as saying. "You can make the title long and scientific-sounding. That's one way."

But Large was skeptical of the program's critics, observing that "there's a built-in yahoo streak in Congress, as there is latent yahooism in us all." Perhaps there is a need for a little more yahooism in Congress, if that's what it takes to bring a little common sense to such spending programs.

A frequent argument for these special currency programs is that the money for the research project is going to benefit the host country. This is true only in part. Once the study is approved, the Smithsonian awards its grant to a U.S. academic institution to undertake the study and American researchers and scientists who conduct the investigations abroad are well paid. A Smithsonian paper on its program explains: "Once our embassies' and the host countries' concurrence has been received, the Smithsonian asks the embassy to disburse funds according to the approved plan of the grantee institution in the United States. Funds usually are paid to the American principal investigator; they are also paid to the local collaborating institution which keeps the accounts, provides the laboratory space and the services of staff scientists and technicians. . . ."

My selection of the Smithsonian's foreign research program is not meant to imply that it alone is guilty of wasting these government funds. The National Science Foundation spent $21,000 on the "Investigation of Mating Calls and Paratoid Gland Secretions of the Central American Toad" and $70,000 on a study of Indo-Australian ants. And the Agriculture Department spent $20,000 on the blood groups of Polish Zlotnika pigs and $29,361 on an odor-measuring machine developed and purchased for Turkey. The eight other federal agencies expending money under the excess foreign currency program should be similarly examined with a fine-tooth comb. But the Smithsonian grant projects, I believe, are highly indicative of the type of government spending that must be stopped.

The case for scientific inquiry could no doubt be made for any subject under the sun, even the Smithsonian's proposed $85,000 study of the impact of rural road construction in Poland. But the American taxpayer is nearing the end of his own road as far as what he is willing to support in the way of government spending. Eventually, taxpayers will, one prays, make it abundantly clear to Washington and to Congress that they have had enough. But when?

Appendix

Alphabetical List of Federal Advisory Committees as of December 31, 1973

Abbreviations

THE PARENTHETICAL ABBREVIATIONS AFTER EACH COMMITTEE listing refer to the following agencies, departments, and selected committees, commissions, and councils:

AC	Administrative Conference of the U.S.
ACDA	U.S. Arms Control and Disarmament Agency
ACFP	Advisory Committee on Federal Pay
ACHP	Advisory Council on Historic Preservation
ACT	ACTION
AEC	Atomic Energy Commission
AGPR	Ad Hoc Advisory Group on Puerto Rico
AID	Agency for International Development
ARBA	American Revolution Bicentennial Administration
CAB	Civil Aeronautics Board
CCOSSP	Cabinet Committee on Opportunities for Spanish Speaking People

CCR	U.S. Commission on Civil Rights
CEA	Council of Economic Advisers
CEQ	Council on Environmental Quality
CLC	Cost of Living Council
COGCFP	Commission on the Organization of the Government for the Conduct of Foreign Policy
CPSC	Consumer Product Safety Commission
CSC	U.S. Civil Service Commission
DOC	Department of Commerce
DOD	Department of Defense
DOI	Department of Interior
DOJ	Department of Justice
DOL	Department of Labor
DOS	Department of State
DOT	Department of Transportation
EIB	Export-Import Bank of the United States
EPA	Environmental Protection Agency
FCC	Federal Communications Commission
FEO	Federal Energy Office
FHLBB	Federal Home Loan Bank Board
FMCS	Federal Mediation and Conciliation Service
FPC	Federal Power Commission
GSA	General Services Administration
HEW	Department of Health, Education and Welfare
HUD	Department of Housing and Urban Development
ICC	Interstate Commerce Commission
NASA	National Aeronautics and Space Administration
NCUA	National Credit Union Administration
NEA	National Endowment for the Arts
NEH	National Endowment for the Humanities
NPTG	Commission on the Review of the National Policy Toward Gambling
NSF	National Science Foundation
ODAP	Office of Drug Abuse Prevention
OMB	Office of Management and Budget
OTP	Office of Telecommunications Policy
RRB	Railroad Retirement Board
SBA	Small Business Administration
SEC	Securities and Exchange Commission
TRES	Department of the Treasury
USDA	Department of Agriculture
USIA	U.S. Information Agency
VA	Veterans Administration
WES	National Commission for the Review of Federal and State Laws

Relating to Wiretapping and Electronic Surveillance
WRC   U.S. Water Resources Council

Federal Advisory Committees

Academic Advisory Board to the Superintendent, U.S. Naval Academy (DOD)
Actuarial Advisory Committee (RRB)
Ad Hoc Advisory Group on Puerto Rico (AGPR)
Ad Hoc Committee for the Evaluation of the Apollo-Soyuz Test Program (ASTP) Experiment Proposals (NASA)
Ad Hoc Synthesis Review Panel for the Evaluation of Lunar Data Analysis and Synthesis Proposals (NASA)
Administrative Conference of the United States (AC)
Administrator's Advisory Committee on Cemeteries and Memorials (VA)
Administrator's Education and Rehabilitation Advisory Committee (VA)
Adult Development and Aging Research Committee (HEW)
Advanced Logistics System Project Advisory Committee (DOD)
Advanced Missile Materials Research Technology Advisory Group (DOD)
Advisory Board for the National Insurance Development Program (HUD)
Advisory Board of the St. Lawrence Seaway Development Corporation (DOT)
Advisory Board on National Parks, Historic Sites, Buildings and Monuments (DOI)
Advisory Board on the San Jose Mission National Historic Site (DOI)
Advisory Board to the U.S. Merchant Marine Academy (DOC)
Advisory Committee for Foreign Service Institute (DOS)
Advisory Committee for National Dredging Study (DOD)
Advisory Committee for Planning and Institutional Affairs (NSF)
Advisory Committee for Radiation Biology Aspects of the SST (DOT)
Advisory Committee for Research (NSF)
Advisory Committee for Research Applications Policy (NSF)
Advisory Committee for Saint-Gaudens National Historic Site (DOI)
Advisory Committee for Science Education (NSF)
Advisory Committee for Statistical Research to the Civil Aeronautics Board, American Statistical Association (CAB)
Advisory Committee for the U.S. Meat Animal Research Center (USDA)
Advisory Committee of the Export-Import Bank of the United States (EIB)
Advisory Committee on Accreditation and Institutional Eligibility (HEW)
Advisory Committee on Alternative Automotive Power Systems (CEQ)
Advisory Committee on Coal Mine Safety Research (DOI)
Advisory Committee on Construction Safety and Health (DOL)
Advisory Committee on Cooperative Work with State Departments of Agriculture (USDA)
Advisory Committee on Ethical and Human Value Implications of Science and Technology (NSF)

Advisory Committee on Explosives Tagging (TRES)
Advisory Committee on Federal Pay (ACFP)
Advisory Committee on Foreign Animal and Poultry Diseases (USDA)
Advisory Committee on "Foreign Relations of the United States" (DOS)
Advisory Committee on GNP Data Improvement (OMB)
Advisory Committee on Grains-Wheat, Feed Grains and Soybeans (USDA)
Advisory Committee on High-Speed Ground Transportation (DOT)
Advisory Committee on Hog Cholera Eradication (USDA)
Advisory Committee on International Business Problems (DOS)
Advisory Committee on International Intellectual Property (DOS)
Advisory Committee on International Organizations (DOS)
Advisory Committee on Meat and Poultry Inspection (USDA)
Advisory Committee on Medical Uses of Isotopes (AEC)
Advisory Committee on Medicare Administration Contracting and
    Subcontracting (HEW)
Advisory Committee on Model Compliance Program for Broker-Dealers
    (SEC)
Advisory Committee on Plant and Nuclear Materials Security (AEC)
Advisory Committee on Reactor Safeguards (AEC)
Advisory Committee on Reform of the International Monetary System
    (TRES)
Advisory Committee on Science and Foreign Affairs (DOS)
Advisory Committee on Sheltered Workshops (DOL)
Advisory Committee on State and Private Forestry (USDA)
Advisory Committee on Structural Safety of Veterans Administration
    Facilities (VA)
Advisory Committee on the Air Force Historical Program (DOD)
Advisory Committee on the Design and Construction of Shelters (DOD)
Advisory Committee on the Economic Role of Women (CEA)
Advisory Committee on the Education of Bilingual Children (HEW)
Advisory Committee on the Law of the Sea (DOS)
Advisory Committee on the Revision and Application of Drinking Water
    Standards (EPA)
Advisory Committee on Transportation-Related Signs and Symbols (DOT)
Advisory Committee on Voluntary Foreign Aid (AID)
Advisory Committee on Water Data for Public Use (DOI)
Advisory Committee on Women to the Secretary of Labor (DOL)
Advisory Committee to the Director, NIH (HEW)
Advisory Committee to the United States National Section of the Inter-
    American Tropical Tuna Commission (DOS)
Advisory Committee to United States Section, International North Pacific
    Fisheries Commission (DOS)
Advisory Council for Minority Enterprise (DOC)
Advisory Council on Developing Institutions (HEW)
Advisory Council on Employee Welfare and Pension Benefit Plans (DOL)

Advisory Council on Financial Aid to Students (HEW)
Advisory Council on Historic Preservation (ACHP)
Advisory Council on Intergovernmental Personnel Policy (CSC)
1974 Advisory Council on Social Security (HEW)
Advisory Council on Spanish Speaking Americans (CCOSSP)
Advisory Council on Urban Transportation (DOT)
Advisory Group to the Commissioner of Internal Revenue (TRES)
Advisory Panel for Anthropology (NSF)
Advisory Panel for Astronomy (NSF)
Advisory Panel for Atmospheric Sciences (NSF)
Advisory Panel for Biochemistry (NSF)
Advisory Panel for Biophysics (NSF)
Advisory Panel for Chemistry (NSF)
Advisory Panel for Computer Science and Engineering (NSF)
Advisory Panel for Developmental Biology (NSF)
Advisory Panel for Earth Sciences (NSF)
Advisory Panel for Economics (NSF)
Advisory Panel for Electrical Sciences and Analysis (NSF)
Advisory Panel for Engineering Chemistry and Energetics (NSF)
Advisory Panel for Engineering Materials (NSF)
Advisory Panel for Engineering Mechanics (NSF)
Advisory Panel for Environmental Biology (NSF)
Advisory Panel for Experimental R&D Incentives (NSF)
Advisory Panel for Genetic Biology (NSF)
Advisory Panel for History and Philosophy of Science (NSF)
Advisory Panel for Human Cell Biology (NSF)
Advisory Panel for Mathematical Sciences (NSF)
Advisory Panel for Metabolic Biology (NSF)
Advisory Panel for Neurobiology (NSF)
Advisory Panel for Oceanography (NSF)
Advisory Panel for Physics (NSF)
Advisory Panel for Political Science (NSF)
Advisory Panel for Psychobiology (NSF)
Advisory Panel for Regulatory Biology (NSF)
Advisory Panel for Research Management Improvement (NSF)
Advisory Panel for Social Psychology (NSF)
Advisory Panel for Sociology (NSF)
Advisory Panel for Systematic Biology (NSF)
Advisory Panel on Academic Music (DOS)
Advisory Panel on Dance (DOS)
Advisory Panel on Drama (DOS)
Advisory Panel on Folk Music and Jazz (DOS)
Advisory Panel on International Law (DOS)
Advisory Panel on Music (DOS)
Advisory Panel on ROTC Affairs (DOD)

Advisory Panel on the Materials Research Laboratories (NSF)
Aerospace Safety Advisory Panel (NASA)
Agricultural Research Policy Advisory Committee (USDA)
Agricultural Research Program and Facilities Subcommittee of Agricultural
   Research Policy Advisory Committee (USDA)
Agriculture Advisory Committee (FEO)
A.I.D. Research Advisory Committee (AID)
Air Force Logistics Command Advisory Board (DOD)
Air Force ROTC Advisory Panel (DOD)
Air Pollution Chemistry and Physics Advisory Committee (EPA)
Air Traffic Control Advisory Committees* (DOT)
Aircraft Structural Integrity Program Industry Advisory Committee (DOD)
ALASKA POWER SURVEY (FPC):
   Executive Advisory Committee
   Technical Advisory Committee on Coordinated System Development and
      Interconnections
   Technical Advisory Committee on Economic Analysis and Load Projection
   Technical Advisory Committee on Environmental Considerations and
      Consumer Affairs
   Technical Advisory Committee on Resources and Electric Power
      Generation
Alcohol Training Review Committee (HEW)
Alcoholism and Alcohol-Problems Review Committee (HEW)
Allergy and Immunology Research Committee (HEW)
Allergy and Immunology Study Section (HEW)
American Bankers Association Government Borrowing Committee (TRES)
American Statistical Association Advisory Committee on Statistical Policy
   (OMB)
Americana Committee for the National Archives (GSA)
Animal Resources Advisory Committee (HEW)
Annual Regulations Conference for Migratory Shore and Upland Game Birds
   (DOI)
Anti-Infective Agents Advisory Committee (HEW)
Antimicrobial Program Advisory Committee (EPA)
Apache National Forest Grazing Advisory Board (USDA)
Apache National Forest Multiple Use Advisory Committee (USDA)
Appalachian National Scenic Trail Advisory Council (DOI)
Applied Physiology and Bioengineering Study Section (HEW)
Arapaho National Forest Multiple Use Advisory Committee (USDA)
Architecture and Environmental Arts Advisory Panel (NEA)
Armed Forces Epidemiological Board (DOD)
Armed Forces Institute of Pathology Scientific Advisory Board (DOD)

---

* Fourteen separate committees.

Army Advisory Panel on ROTC Affairs (DOD)
Army-Air Force Exchange Service Civilian Advisory Committee (DOD)
Army Scientific Advisory Panel (DOD)
Art Advisory Panel of the Commissioner of Internal Revenue (TRES)
Arteriosclerosis Research Centers Advisory Committee (HEW)
Artificial Kidney-Chronic Uremia Advisory Committee (HEW)
Ashley National Forest Cattle Advisory Board (USDA)
Ashley National Forest (Uinta) Woolgrowers' Advisory Board (USDA)
Atomic Energy Labor-Management Advisory Committee (AEC)
Automation in the Medical Laboratory Sciences Review Committee (HEW)

Bacteriology and Mycology Study Section (HEW)
Ballistic Research Laboratories Scientific Advisory Committee (DOD)
Basic Steel Industry Advisory Committee on Apprenticeship and Training
    (DOL)
Behavioral Sciences Research Contract Review Committee (HEW)
Bighorn National Forest Grazing Advisory Board (USDA)
Bighorn National Forest Multiple Use Advisory Committee (USDA)
Biochemistry Study Section (HEW)
Biomedical Communications Study Section (HEW)
Biomedical Library Review Committee (HEW)
Biometric and Epidemiological Methodology Advisory Committee (HEW)
Biometry and Epidemiology Contract Review Committee (HEW)
Biophysics and Biophysical Chemistry A Study Section (HEW)
Biophysics and Biophysical Chemistry B Study Section (HEW)
Bladder-Prostate Cancer Advisory Committee (HEW)
Board of Advisors, Federal Reformatory for Women—Bureau of Prisons
    (DOJ)
Board of Advisors, Industrial College of the Armed Forces (DOD)
Board of Advisors to the Fund for the Improvement of Postsecondary
    Education (HEW)
Board of Advisors to the President, Naval War College (DOD)
Board of Advisors to the Superintendent, Naval Postgraduate School (DOD)
Board of Consultants, The National War College (DOD)
Board of Regents of National Library of Medicine (HEW)
Board of Scientific Counselors, NAIMDD (HEW)
Board of Scientific Counselors, NCI (HEW)
Board of Scientific Counselors, NEI (HEW)
Board of Scientific Counselors, NHLI (HEW)
Board of Scientific Counselors, NIAID (HEW)
Board of Scientific Counselors, NICHD (HEW)
Board of Scientific Counselors, NIDR (HEW)
Board of Scientific Counselors, NIEHS (HEW)
Board of Scientific Counselors, NIMH (HEW)

Board of Scientific Counselors, NINDS (HEW)
Board of Tea Experts (HEW)
Board of Visitors, Air University (DOD)
Board of Visitors, Defense Intelligence School (DOD)
Board of Visitors, Defense Systems Management School (DOD)
Board of Visitors, Judge Advocate General's School (DOD)
Board of Visitors, U.S. Air Force Academy (DOD)
Board of Visitors, U.S. Military Academy (DOD)
Board of Visitors, U.S. Naval Academy (DOD)
Boating Safety Advisory Council (DOT)
Boise National Forest Livestock Advisory Board (USDA)
Bonneville Regional Advisory Council (DOI)
Breast Cancer Diagnosis Committee (HEW)
Breast Cancer Epidemiology Committee (HEW)
Breast Cancer Experimental Biology Committee (HEW)
Breast Cancer Treatment Committee (HEW)
Business Advisory Committee (FEO)
Business Advisory Committee on Federal Reports (OMB)
Business Research Advisory Council and its Committees (DOL)
    Committee on Consumer and Wholesale Prices
    Committee on Economic Trends and Labor Conditions
    Committee on Foreign Labor and Trade
    Committee on Manpower and Employment
    Committee on Occupational Safety and Health
    Committee on Productivity and Technological Developments
    Committee on Wages and Industrial Relations

CAB Industry Advisory Committee on Aviation Mobilization (CAB)
Cable Technical Advisory Committee (FCC)
Cable Television Advisory Committee on Federal/State Local Relations
    (FCC)
California Advisory Committee to the U.S. Forest Service (USDA)
California Regional Roads Committee (USDA)
Cancer Clinical Investigation Review Committee (HEW)
Cancer Control Advisory Committee (HEW)
Cancer Control Education Review Committee (HEW)
Cancer Control Prevention and Detection Review Committee (HEW)
Cancer Control Treatment and Rehabilitation Review Committee (HEW)
Cancer Research Center Review Committee (HEW)
Cancer Special Program Advisory Committee (HEW)
Cancer Treatment Advisory Committee (HEW)
Cape Cod National Seashore Advisory Commission (DOI)
Cardiovascular and Pulmonary Study Section (HEW)
Cardiovascular and Renal Advisory Committee (HEW)

Cardiovascular and Renal Study Section (HEW)
Career Development Committee (VA)
Caribou National Forest Grazing Advisory Board (USDA)
Carrizo Grazing Advisory Board, San Isabel National Forest (USDA)
Carson National Forest Multiple Use Advisory Committee (USDA)
Cell Biology Study Section (HEW)
Census Advisory Committee of the American Economic Association (DOC)
Census Advisory Committee of the American Marketing Association (DOC)
Census Advisory Committee of the American Statistical Association (DOC)
Census Advisory Committee on Agriculture Statistics (DOC)
Census Advisory Committee on Population Statistics (DOC)
Census Advisory Committee on Privacy and Confidentiality (DOC)
Census Advisory Committee on Small Areas (DOC)
Census Advisory Committee on State and Local Government Statistics (DOC)
Center for Building Technology Advisory Committee (DOC)
Central Office Education and Training Review Panel (VA)
CEQ Governor's Advisory Committee on the Environmental Impacts of
    Potential OCS Oil and Gas Development (CEQ)
Challis National Forest Livestock Advisory Board (USDA)
Chemical/Biological Information-Handling Review Committee (HEW)
Chesapeake and Ohio Canal National Historical Park Commission (DOI)
Chief Medical Director's Ad Hoc Advisory Committee on Spinal Cord Injury
    (VA)
Cibola National Forest Grazing Advisory Board (USDA)
Cibola National Forest Multiple Use Advisory Committee (USDA)
Citizens' Advisory Committee on Civil Rights (USDA)
Citizens' Advisory Committee on Environmental Quality (CEQ)
Citizens' Advisory Committee on Transportation Quality (DOT)
Citizens' Advisory Council on the Status of Women (DOL)
Civilian Advisory Board, Chief of Naval Personnel (DOD)
Clinical Program-Projects Research Review Committee (HEW)
Clinical Projects Research Review Committee (HEW)
Clinical Psychopharmacology Research Review Committee (HEW)
CNO Executive Panel Advisory Committee (DOD)
CNO Industry Advisory Committee for Telecommunications (DOD)
Coal Mine Health Research Advisory Council (HEW)
Coast Guard Science Advisory Committee (DOT)
Coastal Engineering Research Board (DOD)
Coastal Zone Management Advisory Committee (DOC)
Coconino National Forest Grazing Advisory Board (USDA)
Coconino National Forest Multiple Use Advisory Committee (USDA)
Coins and Medals Advisory Panel (ARBA)
Colon-Rectum Cancer Advisory Committee (HEW)
Commandant's Advisory Committee on Marine Corps History (DOD)
Commemorations and Convocations Advisory Panel

(Ad Hoc Special Subcommittee on Commemorations) (ARBA)
Commerce Technical Advisory Board (DOC)
Commission on the Organization of the Government for the Conduct of
     Foreign Policy
Commission on the Review of the National Policy Toward Gambling
     (NPTG)
Commission on the Revision of the Federal Court Appellate System (DOJ)
Committee for the Preservation of the White House (DOI)
Committee for the Recovery of Archeological Remains (DOI)
Committee of Nine (USDA)
Committee of Senior Reviewers (AEC)
Committee on Cancer Immunobiology (HEW)
Committee on Cancer Immunodiagnosis (HEW)
Committee on Cancer Immunotherapy (HEW)
Committee on Cytology Automation (HEW)
Committee on Federal Laboratories (NSF)
Committee on Minority Participation in Earth Science and Mineral
     Engineering (DOI)
Committee on Private Voluntary Agency Eligibility (CSC)
Committee on the Immunology of Cancer Cause and Prevention (HEW)
Commodity Credit Corporation Advisory Board (USDA)

Communicative Disorders Review Committee (HEW)
Communicative Sciences Study Section (HEW)
Community College of the Air Force Advisory Committee (DOD)
Computer and Biomathematical Sciences Study Section (HEW)
Computer Peripherals, Components, and Test Equipment Technical Advisory
     Committee (DOC)
Computer Systems Technical Advisory Committee (DOC)
Condor Advisory Committee (USDA)
Consulting Committee for the National Survey of Historic Sites and Buildings
     (DOI)
Consulting Committee of Bank Economists (TRES)
Consumer Advisory Committee (FEO)
Consumer Advisory Council (HEW)
Continuing Education Training Review Committee (HEW)
Contraceptive Development Contract Review Committee (HEW)
Contraceptive Evaluation Research Contract Review Committee (HEW)
Controlled Substances Advisory Committee (HEW)
Cooperative Forestry Research Advisory Board (USDA)
Cooperative Forestry Research Advisory Committee (USDA)
Cooperative Studies Evaluation Committee (VA)
Coronado National Forest Grazing Advisory Board (USDA)
Coronado National Forest Multiple Use Advisory Committee (USDA)
Cradle of Forestry in America Advisory Committee (USDA)
Creative and Visual Arts Advisory Panel (ARBA)

Crime and Delinquency Review Committee (HEW)

Dance Advisory Panel (NEA)
Defense Advisory Committee on Women in the Services (DOD)
Defense Science Board (DOD)
Dental Caries Program Advisory Committee (HEW)
Dental Drug Products Advisory Committee (HEW)
Dental Research Institutes and Special Programs Advisory Committee
    (HEW)
Dental Study Section (HEW)
Department of the Army Historical Advisory Committee (DOD)
Dermatology Advisory Committee (HEW)
Descanso District Grazing Advisory Board, Cleveland National Forest
    (USDA)
Deschutes National Forest Advisory Committee (USDA)
Deschutes National Forest Cattlemen's and Woolgrowers' Grazing Advisory
    Board (USDA)
Developmental Behavior Sciences Study Section (HEW)
Diagnostic Products Advisory Committee (HEW)
Diagnostic Radiology Committee (HEW)
Diagnostic Research Advisory Group (HEW)
Distributors' Advisory Committee (USDA)
District Advisory Committees* (SBA)
DOD Advisory Group on Electron Devices (DOD)
DOD Hemoglobinopathy Policy Review Committee (DOD)
DOD High-Energy Laser Review Group (DOD)
DOD-Industry Integrated Logistic Support Advisory Committee (DOD)
DOD Wage Committee (DOD)
Drug Experience Advisory Committee (HEW)

Earthquake Studies Advisory Panel (DOI)
Economic Advisory Board (DOC)
Education Panel (NEH)
Effluent Standards and Water Quality Information Advisory Committee
    (EPA)
Electromagnetic Radiation Management Advisory Council (OTP)
Electromagnetic Reception Advisory Panel (DOD)
Electronic Data Processing Advisory Panel (DOD)
Electronic Instrumentation Technical Advisory Committee (DOC)
Electronics Advisory Group, U.S. Army Electronics Command (DOD)
Emergency Advisory Committee for Natural Gas (DOI)
Emergency Economic Stabilization Industry Advisory Committee for Food
    Retailing (GSA)

---

* Sixty-four separate committees.

Emergency Economic Stabilization Industry Advisory Committee for Food Service (GSA)

Emergency Economic Stabilization Industry Advisory Committee for Lumber and Wood Products (GSA)

Emergency Economic Stabilization Industry Advisory Committee for Retailing (other than food & automobiles) (GSA)

Emergency Medical Services Administrator's Advisory Committee (HEW)

Emergency Petroleum Supply Committee (DOI)

Employee Advisory Committee on Health Benefits (CSC)

Endocrinology and Metabolism Advisory Committee (HEW)

Endocrinology Study Section (HEW)

Engineering, Architectural and Construction Industry Advisory Committee (AID)

Engineers Environmental Advisory Committee, Chief of Engineers (DOD)

English Teaching Advisory Panel (USIA)

Environmental Advisory Committee (FEO)

Environmental Radiation Exposure Advisory Committee (EPA)

Epidemiologic Studies Review Committee (HEW)

Epidemiology and Biometry Advisory Committee (HEW)

Epidemiology and Disease Control Study Section (HEW)

Epilepsy Advisory Committee (HEW)

Expansion Arts Advisory Panel (NEA)

Experimental and Special Training Review Committee (HEW)

Experimental Psychology Research Review Committee (HEW)

Experimental Psychology Study Section (HEW)

Experimental Therapeutics Study Section (HEW)

Expert Panel on Nitrites and Nitrosamines (USDA)

Exporters' Textile Advisory Committee (DOC)

FDA-NIMH Drug Abuse Advisory Committee (HEW)

Federal Advisory Council on Employment Security (DOL)

Federal Advisory Council on Unemployment Insurance (DOL)

Federal Architecture Task Force Advisory Panel (NEA)

Federal Committee on Apprenticeship (DOL)

Federal Council on the Aging (HEW)

Federal Employees Pay Council (CSC/OMB)
   (Director, Office of Management and Budget, and Chairman, U.S. Civil Service Commission, serve jointly as President's agent for this Council.)

Federal Graphics Evaluation Advisory Panel (NEA)

Federal Hospital Council (HEW)

Federal Information Processing Standards (FIPS) Coordinating and Advisory Committee (DOC)

Federal Prevailing Rate Advisory Committee (CSC)

Federal Safety Advisory Council (DOL)

Federal Savings and Loan Advisory Council (FHLBB)
Federal-State/Special Projects Advisory Panel (NEA)
Fellowships Panel (NEH)
Festival USA Program Committee (ARBA)
Fine Arts Committee (DOS)
FIPS Task Group 12 (Significance and Impact of ASCII as a Federal
   Standard) (DOC)
FIPS Task Group 13 (Workload Definition and Benchmark) (DOC)
Flight Information Advisory Committee (DOT)
Flood Insurance Advisory Committee (HUD)
Food Industry Advisory Committee (CLC)
Food Industry Wage and Salary Committee (CLC)
Foreign Petroleum Supply Committee (DOI)
Forest Research Advisory Committee (Orono, Maine) (USDA)
Fremont National Forest Grazing Advisory Board (USDA)
Frequency Management Advisory Council (OTP)
Fund Raising Advisory Council (CSC)

Gateway National Recreation Area Advisory Commission (DOI)
General Advisory Committee (AEC)
General Advisory Committee on Arms Control and Disarmament (ACDA)
General Aviation Accident Prevention Industry Advisory Committee (DOT)
General Clinical Research Centers Committee (HEW)
General Medicine A Study Section (HEW)
General Medicine B Study Section (HEW)
General Research Support Program Advisory Committee (HEW)
General Services Administration Special Study Committee on the Selection of
   Architects and Engineers (GSA)
General Services Public Advisory Council (GSA)
General Technical Advisory Committee (DOI)
Genetics Study Section (HEW)
Gila National Forest Grazing Advisory Board (USDA)
Golden Gate National Recreation Area Advisory Commission (DOI)
Government Advisory Committee on International Book and Library
   Programs (DOS)
Grand Mesa and Uncompahgre National Forests Multiple Use Advisory
   Committee (USDA)
Grand Mesa National Forest Grazing Advisory Board (USDA)
Grazing District Advisory Boards (53 each) (DOI)
Great Lakes Pilotage Advisory Committee (DOT)
Great Plains States Regional Manpower Advisory Committee (DOL)
Gulf Islands National Seashore Advisory Commission (DOI)
Gunnison National Forest Multiple Use Advisory Committee (USDA)
Gunnison Valley Forest Grazing Advisory Board (USDA)

Harry Diamond Laboratories Scientific Advisory Committee (DOD)
Hazardous Materials Advisory Committee (EPA)
Health Care Technology Study Section (HEW)
Health Industry Advisory Committee (CLC)
Health Industry Wage and Salary Committee (CLC)
Health Insurance Benefits Advisory Council (HEW)
Health Services Developmental Grants Study Section (HEW)
Health Services Research Study Section (HEW)
Health Services Research Training Committee (HEW)
Heart and Lung Program-Project Committee (HEW)
Hematology Study Section (HEW)
Heritage '76 Program Committee (ARBA)
High Energy Physics Advisory Panel (AEC)
Historic American Buildings Survey Advisory Board (DOI)
Historic American Engineering Record Advisory Committee (DOI)
Historic Conservation Advisory Panel (ARBA)
Historical Advisory Committee (AEC)
Honokohau Study Advisory Commission (DOI)
Hop Marketing Advisory Board (USDA)
Horizons '76 Advisory Group (ARBA)
Horizons '76 Program Committee (ARBA)
Hot Springs National Park Examining Board for Technicians (DOI)
Hot Springs National Park Registration Board (DOI)
Human Embryology and Development Study Section (HEW)
Hypertension Information and Education Advisory Committee (HEW)
Hypertension Research Centers Advisory Committee (HEW)

Immunization Practices Advisory Committee (HEW)
Immunobiology Study Section (HEW)
Importers' Textile Advisory Committee (DOC)
Independence National Historical Park Advisory Commission (DOI)
Indian Education for Health Committee (DOI)
Indian Health Advisory Committee (HEW)
Indiana Dunes National Lakeshore Advisory Commission (DOI)
Industry Advisory Committee on Coal Exports (DOI)
Industry Advisory Committee on Metal Scrap Problems (DOC)
Industry Advisory Committee to the Defense Electric Power Administration
   (DOI)
Industry Advisory Council (DOD)
Infectious Disease Committee (HEW)
International Decade of Ocean Exploration Advisory Panel (NSF)
International Decade of Ocean Exploration Proposal Review Panel (NSF)
Investment Securities Advisory Committee (TRES)
Invitation to the World Advisory Panel (ARBA)

186

Joint Commission on the Coinage (TRES)
Joint Federal, State, and Local Government Advisory Panel on Procurement and Supply (GSA)
Joint USDA-National Association of State Departments of Agriculture Committee (USDA)
Junior Science and Humanities Symposia Advisory Committee (DOD)
Juvenile Problems Research Review Committee (HEW)

Klamath National Forest Advisory Board (Grazing) (USDA)
Knowledge and Human Values Panel (NEH)

Labor Advisory Committee on Statistics (OMB)
Labor-Management Advisory Committee (CLC)
Labor Research Advisory Council and its committees (DOL)
    Committee on Foreign Labor and Trade
    Committee on Industrial Safety
    Committee on Manpower and Employment
    Committee on Prices and Living Conditions
    Committee on Productivity, Technology and Growth
    Committee on Wages and Industrial Relations
Lignite Advisory Committee (DOI)
Lincoln National Forest Grazing Advisory Board (USDA)
Lipid Metabolism Advisory Committee (HEW)
Literature Advisory Panel (NEA)
Long-Term Care for the Elderly Research Review and Advisory Committee (HEW)
Lunar Planning Committee (NASA)

Malheur National Forest Grazing Advisory Board (USDA)
Malheur National Forest Multiple Use Advisory Committee (USDA)
Mammalian Mutant Cell Lines Committee (HEW)
Management-Labor Textile Advisory Committee (DOC)
Manti-LaSal National Forest, Manti Division Advisory Board (USDA)
Mar-A-Lago National Historic Site Advisory Commission (DOI)
Marine Fisheries Advisory Committee (DOC)
Marine Safety Council Chemical Transportation Industry Advisory Committee (DOT)
Marine Safety Council Industry Advisory Committee on Rules of the Road (DOT)
Marine Safety Council National Offshore Operations Industry Advisory Committee (DOT)
Marine Safety Council Towing Industry Advisory Committee (DOT)
Maritime Policy Industry Advisory Committee (DOD)
Maternal and Child Health Research Committee (HEW)

Maternal and Child Health Service Research Grants Review Committee (HEW)
Medical Devices Advisory Committee (HEW)
Medical Devices Application Committee (HEW)
Medical Isotopes Advisory Subcommittee of the JSC Radiation Safety Committee (NASA)
Medical Laboratory Services Advisory Committee (HEW)
Medical Radiation Advisory Committee (HEW)
Medicinal Chemistry A Study Section (HEW)
Medicinal Chemistry B Study Section (HEW)
Medicine Bow National Forest Grazing Advisory Board (USDA)
Mental Health Services Research Review Committee (HEW)
Mental Health Small Grant Committee (HEW)
Mental Retardation Research Committee (HEW)
Merit Review Board for Alcoholism and Drug Dependence Programs (VA)
Merit Review Board for Basic Science Programs (VA)
Merit Review Board for Behavioral Science Programs (VA)
Merit Review Board for Cardiovascular Programs (VA)
Merit Review Board for Endocrinology Programs (VA)
Merit Review Board for Gastroenterology Programs (VA)
Merit Review Board for Hematology Programs (VA)
Merit Review Board for Immunology Programs (VA)
Merit Review Board for Infectious Disease Programs (VA)
Merit Review Board for Nephrology Programs (VA)
Merit Review Board for Neurobiology Programs (VA)
Merit Review Board for Oncology Programs (VA)
Merit Review Board for Oral Biology Programs (VA)
Merit Review Board for Respiration Programs (VA)
Merit Review Board for Surgery Programs (VA)
Metabolism Study Section (HEW)
Meteorology Advisory Committee (EPA)
Metropolitan Mental Health Problems Review Committee (HEW)
Microbial Chemistry Study Section (HEW)
Microwave Landing System Advisory Committee (DOT)
Middle Atlantic Regional Manpower Advisory Committee (DOL)
Miguel District Grazing Advisory Board, Grand Mesa-Uncompahgre National Forests (USDA)
Military Airlift Committee of the National Defense Transportation Association (DOD)
Mills Grazing Advisory Board, Cibola National Forest (USDA)
Minority Mental Health Advisory Committee (HEW)
Minute Man National Historical Park Advisory Commission (DOI)
Modoc National Forest Grazing Advisory Board (USDA)
Molecular Biology Study Section (HEW)
Molecular Control Working Group (HEW)

Monongahela National Forest Advisory Committee (USDA)
Montezuma Section, San Juan National Forest Grazing Advisory Board (USDA)
Mountain States Regional Manpower Advisory Committee (DOL)
Museum Advisory Panel (NEA)
Music Advisory Panel (NEA)

Narcotic Addiction and Drug Abuse Review Committee (HEW)
NASA Historical Advisory Committee (NASA)
NASA Wage Committee (NASA)
National Advisory Allergy and Infectious Diseases Council (HEW)
National Advisory Board Council (DOI)
National Advisory Board for Wild Free-Roaming Horses and Burros (DOI)
National Advisory Child Health and Human Development Council (HEW)
National Advisory Commission on Multiple Sclerosis (HEW)
National Advisory Committee for the Flammable Fabrics Act (CPSC)
National Advisory Committee on Banking Policies and Practices (TRES)
National Advisory Committee on Occupational Safety and Health (DOL)
National Advisory Committee on Oceans and Atmosphere (DOC)
National Advisory Committee on the Handicapped (HEW)
National Advisory Committee on Uniform Traffic Control Devices (DOT)
National Advisory Council (SBA)
National Advisory Council for Drug Abuse Prevention (ODAP)
National Advisory Council on Adult Education (HEW)
National Advisory Council on Alcohol Abuse and Alcoholism (HEW)
National Advisory Council on Child Nutrition (USDA)
National Advisory Council on Comprehensive Health Planning Programs (HEW)
National Advisory Council on Drug Abuse (HEW)
National Advisory Council on Education of Disadvantaged Children (HEW)
National Advisory Council on Education Professions Development (HEW)
National Advisory Council on Equality of Educational Opportunity (HEW)
National Advisory Council on Ethnic Heritage Studies (HEW)
National Advisory Council on Extension and Continuing Education (HEW)
National Advisory Council on Health Manpower Shortage Areas (HEW)
National Advisory Council on Health Professions Education (HEW)
National Advisory Council on Health Research Facilities (HEW)
National Advisory Council on Indian Education (HEW)
National Advisory Council on Nurse Training (HEW)
National Advisory Council on Regional Medical Programs (HEW)
National Advisory Council on Services and Facilities for the Developmentally Disabled (HEW)
National Advisory Council on Supplementary Centers and Services (HEW)
National Advisory Council on Vocational Education (HEW)
National Advisory Dental Research Council (HEW)

National Advisory Drug Committee (HEW)
National Advisory Environmental Health Sciences Council (HEW)
National Advisory Eye Council (HEW)
National Advisory Food Committee (HEW)
National Advisory General Medical Sciences Council (HEW)
National Advisory Health Council (HEW)
National Advisory Health Services Council (HEW)
National Advisory Mental Health Council (HEW)
National Advisory Neurological Diseases and Stroke Council (HEW)
National Advisory Public Health Training Council (HEW)
National Advisory Research Resources Council (HEW)
National Advisory Veterinary Medicine Committee (HEW)
National Air Pollution Control Techniques Advisory Committee (EPA)
National Air Pollution Manpower Development Advisory Committee (EPA)
National Air Quality Criteria Advisory Committee (EPA)
National Arboretum Advisory Council (USDA)
National Archives Advisory Council (GSA)
National Arthritis, Metabolism and Digestive Diseases Advisory Council
    (HEW)
National Blood Resource Program Advisory Committee (HEW)
National Board for the Promotion of Rifle Practice (DOD)
National Bureau of Standards Visiting Committee (DOC)
National Business Council for Consumer Affairs (NBCCA) (DOC)
National Cancer Advisory Board (HEW)
National Capital Memorial Advisory Committee (DOI)
National Commission for Industrial Peace (CLC)
National Commission for Manpower Policy (DOL)
National Commission for the Review of Federal and State Laws Relating to
    Wiretapping and Electronic Surveillance (WES)
National Committee for Employer Support of the Guard and Reserve (DOD)
National Cotton Advisory Committee (USDA)
National Council on Indian Opportunity (DOI)
National Council on Quality in Education (HEW)
National Council on the Arts (NEA)
National Council on the Humanities (NEH)
National Credit Union Board (NCUA)
National Crime Information Center Advisory Policy Board—Federal Bureau
    of Investigation (DOJ)
NATIONAL GAS SURVEY (FPC)
    Coordinating Committee Coordinating Task Force
    Distribution Technical Advisory Committee
        Task Force: Facilities
        Task Force: Finance
        Task Force: General
        Task Force: Regulation and Legislation

Executive Advisory Committee
Supply Technical Advisory Committee
    Task Force: Liquefied Natural Gas
    Task Force: Natural Gas Supply
    Task Force: Natural Gas Technology
    Task Force: Reformer Gas
    Task Force: Regulation and Legislation
    Task Force: Synthetic Gas-Coal
Transmission Technical Advisory Committee
    Task Force: Economics
    Task Force: Facilities
    Task Force: Operations
    Task Force: Regulation and Legislation
National Health Resources Advisory Committee (GSA)
National Heart and Lung Advisory Council (HEW)
National Highway Safety Advisory Committee (DOT)
National Horse Industry Advisory Committee (USDA)
National Industrial Energy Conservation Council (DOC)
National Industrial Pollution Control Council (NIPCC) (DOC)
National Industrial Reserve Review Committee (DOD)
National Industry Advisory Committee (FCC)
National Inventors Council (DOC)
National Labor-Management Manpower Policy Committee (GSA)
National Labor-Management Mobilization Planning Committee (DOL)
National Labor-Management Panel (FMCS)
National Magnet Laboratory Visiting Committee (NSF)
National Manpower Advisory Committee and its three subcommittees (DOL)
  Subcommittee on Professional Scientific and Technical Manpower
  Subcommittee on Research, Development and Evaluation
  Subcommittee on Training
National Medical Libraries Assistance Advisory Board (HEW)
National Migrant Health Advisory Committee (HEW)
National Motor Vehicle Safety Advisory Council (DOT)
National Park Service Midwest Regional Advisory Committee (DOI)
National Park Service Northeast Regional Advisory Committee (DOI)
National Park Service Pacific Northwest Regional Advisory Committee
  (DOI)
National Park Service Southeast Regional Advisory Committee (DOI)
National Park Service Southwest Regional Advisory Committee (DOI)
National Park Service Western Regional Advisory Committee (DOI)
National Peanut Advisory Committee (USDA)
National Petroleum Council (DOI)
NATIONAL POWER SURVEY (FPC)
  Coordinating Committee
  Executive Advisory Committee

Technical Advisory Committee on Conservation of Energy
    Task Force on Environmental Aspects
    Task Force on Practices and Standards
    Task Force on Technical Aspects
Technical Advisory Committee on Finance
    Task Force on Future Financial Requirements
Technical Advisory Committee on Fuels
    Task Force—Administrative
    Task Force on Environmental Considerations and Constraints
    Task Force on Fuel Use Alternatives
    Task Force on Utility Fuels Availability
    Task Force on Utility Fuels Requirements
Technical Advisory Committee on Power Supply
    Task Force on Forecast Review
Technical Advisory Committee on Research and Development
    Task Force on Energy Conversion Research
    Task Force on Energy Distribution Research
    Task Force on Energy Sources Research
    Task Force on Energy Systems Research
    Task Force on Environmental Research
National Professional Standards Review Council (HEW)
National Public Advisory Committee on Regional Economic Development (DOC)
National Public Advisory Panel on Architectural and Engineering Services (GSA)
National Review Board Center for Cultural and Technical Interchange Between East and West (DOS)
National Rice Advisory Committee (USDA)
National Rural Fire Defense Committee (USDA)
National Tobacco Advisory Committee (USDA)
National Visitor Facilities Advisory Commission (DOI)
National Voluntary Service Advisory Council (ACT)
Natural Sciences Advisory Committee (DOI)
Naval Research Advisory Committee (DOD)
Navy Resale Advisory Committee (DOD)
Nebraska National Forest Livestock Advisory Board (USDA)
Nectarine Shippers' Advisory Committee (USDA)
Neurological Diseases and Stroke Science Information Program Advisory Committee (HEW)
Neurological Disorders Program-Project Review A Committee (HEW)
Neurological Disorders Program-Project Review B Committee (HEW)
Neurology A Study Section (HEW)
Neurology B Study Section (HEW)
Neuropharmacology Advisory Committee (HEW)
Neuropsychology Research Review Committee (HEW)

New England Regional Manpower Advisory Committee (DOC)
New York Bight MESA Advisory Committee (DOC)
New York Harbor Vessel Traffic System Advisory Committee (DOT)
Nonunion Construction Advisory Committee (CLC)
North Atlantic Regional Manpower Advisory Committee (DOL)
North Central Regional Manpower Advisory Committee (DOL)
North End District Grazing Advisory Board, Grand Mesa-Uncompahgre
    National Forests (USDA)
North Kaibab Grazing Advisory Board (USDA)
Northeastern Forest Research Advisory Committee (USDA)
Northwest Atlantic Fisheries Advisory Committee (DOS)
Norwood District Grazing Advisory Board, Grand Mesa-Uncompahgre
    National Forests (USDA)
NSA Scientific Advisory Board (DOD)
Numerically Controlled Machine Tool Technical Advisory Committee (DOC)
Nursing Research and Education Advisory Committee (HEW)
Nutrition Study Section (HEW)
O and C Advisory Board (DOI)
O and C District Advisory Boards (5 each) (DOI)
Obstetrics and Gynecology Advisory Committee (HEW)
Ocean Affairs Advisory Committee (DOS)
Oceanographic Advisory Committee (DOD)
Ochoco National Forest Multiple Use Advisory Committee (USDA)
OECD Petroleum Advisory Committee (DOI)
Okanogan National Forest Grazing Advisory Board (USDA)
Okanogan National Forest Multiple Use Advisory Committee (USDA)
Oncologic Drugs Advisory Committee (HEW)
Ophthalmic Drugs Advisory Committee (HEW)
Oregon Dunes National Recreation Area Advisory Council (USDA)
Ottawa National Forest Advisory Committee (USDA)
Ouray District Grazing Advisory Board, Grand Mesa-Uncompahgre National
    Forests (USDA)
Outer Planets Science Advisory Committee (NASA)
Overseas Schools Advisory Council (DOS)
Ozark National Scenic Riverways Advisory Commission (DOI)

Pacific Crest National Scenic Trail Advisory Committee (USDA)
Pacific Northwest Forestry Research Advisory Committee (USDA)
Pacific Northwest Regional Manpower Advisory Committee (DOL)
Paint and Varnish Industrial Advisory Committee (EPA)
Panel on Review of Allergenic Extracts (HEW)
Panel on Review of Anesthesiological Devices (HEW)
Panel on Review of Antacids (HEW)
Panel on Review of Antimicrobial Agents (HEW)
Panel on Review of Antiperspirant Drug Products (HEW)
Panel on Review of Bacterial Vaccines and Bacterial Antigens (HEW)

Panel on Review of Bacterial Vaccines and Toxoids (HEW)

Panel on Review of Blood and Blood Derivatives (HEW)

Panel on Review of Cardiovascular Devices (HEW)

Panel on Review of Cold, Cough Allergy, Bronchodilator, and Anti-asthmatic Agents (HEW)

Panel on Review of Contraceptives and Other Vaginal Drug Products (HEW)

Panel on Review of Dental Devices (HEW)

Panel on Review of Dentifrices and Dental Care Agents (HEW)

Panel on Review of Ear, Nose, and Throat Devices (HEW)

Panel on Review of Gastroenterology and Urological Devices (HEW)

Panel on Review of General and Plastic Surgery Devices (HEW)

Panel on Review of General Hospital Devices (HEW)

Panel on Review of Hemorrhoidal Drugs (HEW)

Panel on Review of Immune Serums, Antitoxins, and Antivenins (HEW)

Panel on Review of Internal Analgesic Including Antirheumatic Drugs (HEW)

Panel on Review of In Vitro Diagnostic Reagents (HEW)

Panel on Review of Laxative, Antidiarrheal, Antimetic, and Emetic Drugs (HEW)

Panel on Review of Miscellaneous Biological Products (HEW)

Panel on Review of Miscellaneous External Drug Products (HEW)

Panel on Review of Miscellaneous Internal Drug Products (HEW)

Panel on Review of Neurology Devices (HEW)

Panel on Review of Obstetrics and Gynecology Devices (HEW)

Panel on Review of Ophthalmic Devices (HEW)

Panel on Review of Ophthalmic Drugs (HEW)

Panel on Review of Oral Hygiene Drug Products (HEW)

Panel on Review of Orthopaedic Devices (HEW)

Panel on Review of Pathology Devices (HEW)

Panel on Review of Physiatry Devices (HEW)

Panel on Review of Radiology Devices (HEW)

Panel on Review of Sedative, Tranquilizer, and Sleep Aid Drugs (HEW)

Panel on Review of Skin Test Antigens (HEW)

Panel on Review of Topical Analgesics Including Antirheumatic, Otic, Burn, Sunburn Treatment, and Prevention Drugs (HEW)

Panel on Review of Viral Vaccines and Rickettsial Vaccines (HEW)

Panel on Review of Vitamin, Mineral, and Hematinic Drug Products (HEW)

Paonia Area Forest Grazing Advisory Board, Gunnison National Forest (USDA)

Pathology A Study Section (HEW)

Pathology B Study Section (HEW)

PBX Standards Advisory Committee (FCC)

Peach Sales Managers' Committee (USDA)

Pear Sales Managers' Committee (USDA)

Performing Arts Advisory Panel (ARBA)

Periodontal Diseases Advisory Committee (HEW)

Perishable Agricultural Commodities Act-Industry Advisory Committee (USDA)

Personality and Cognition Research Review Committee (HEW)

Petrochemical Industry Advisory Committee (EPA)

Petroleum Industry Advisory Committee (Independent Sector) (FEO)

Petroleum Security Subcommittee of the Foreign Petroleum Supply Committee (DOI)

Pharmacology Study Section (HEW)

Pharmacology-Toxicology Program Committee (HEW)

Philatelic Advisory Panel (ARBA)

Physiological Chemistry Study Section (HEW)

Physiology Study Section (HEW)

Pictured Rocks National Lakeshore Advisory Commission (DOI)

Pike National Forest Multiple Use Advisory Committee (USDA)

Pipeline Advisory Committee (ICC)

Planning Office Panel (NEH)

Plant Variety Protection Board (USDA)

Plum Sales Managers' Committee (USDA)

Population Research Committee (HEW)

Population Research Study Section (HEW)

Post Viking Mars Science Advisory Committee (NASA)

Preclinical Psychopharmacology Research Review Committee (HEW)

Prescott National Forest Grazing Advisory Board (USDA)

President's Advisory Committee on the Environmental Merit Awards Program (EPA)

President's Air Quality Advisory Board (EPA)

President's Cancer Panel (HEW)

President's Commission on White House Fellows (CSC)

President's Committee on Mental Retardation (HEW)

President's Committee on the National Medal of Science (NSF)

President's Council on Physical Fitness and Sports (HEW)

President's Export Council (DOC)

Primate Research Centers Advisory Committee (HEW)

Private Security Advisory Council (LEAA) (DOJ)

Product Safety Advisory Council (CPSC)

Professional Education Advisory Committee (DOD)

Program Advisory Committee (GSA)

Prologue Editorial Board (GSA)

Public Advisory Committee for Trademark Affairs (DOC)

Public Advisory Committee on Soil and Water Conservation (USDA)

Public Health Conference on Records and Statistics—Standing Committee (HEW)

Public Media Advisory Panel (NEA)

Public Programs Panel (NEH)

Publications and Research Advisory Panel (ARBA)
Pulmonary-Allergy and Clinical Immunology Advisory Committee (HEW)
Pulmonary Diseases Advisory Committee (HEW)

Radiation Bioeffects and Epidemiology Advisory Committee (HEW)
Radiation Study Section (HEW)
Radio Technical Commission for Aeronautics (FCC)
Radio Technical Commission for Marine Services (FCC)
Radioactive Pharmaceuticals Advisory Committee (HEW)
Raisin Advisory Board (USDA)
Regional Advisory Committees on Banking Policies and Practices (fourteen
    separate committees, one for each National Bank Region) (TRES)
Regional Archives Advisory Councils* (GSA)
Regional Public Advisory Panels on Architectural and Engineering Services*
    (GSA)
Reproductive Biology Study Section (HEW)
Research and Technology Advisory Council (RTAC) (NASA)
    Committee on Aeronautical Operating Systems
    Committee on Aeronautical Propulsion
    Committee on Aeronautics
    Committee on Guidance, Control and Information Systems
    Committee on Materials and Structures
    Committee on Research
    Committee on Space Propulsion and Power
    Committee on Space Vehicles
Research Panel (NEH)
Respiratory and Anesthetic Drugs Advisory Committee (HEW)
Rice Inspection Industry Advisory Committee (USDA)
Rio Grande National Forest Grazing Advisory Board (USDA)
Rio Grande National Forest Multiple Use Advisory Committee (USDA)
Rogue River National Forest Grazing Advisory Board (USDA)
Roosevelt Library Editorial Advisory Board (GSA)
Roosevelt National Forest Grazing Advisory Board (USDA)
Roosevelt National Forest Multiple Use Advisory Committee (USDA)
Routt National Forest Grazing Advisory Board (USDA)
Routt National Forest Multiple Use Advisory Committee (USDA)

Safety and Occupational Health Study Section (HEW)
San Isabel National Forest Grazing Advisory Board (USDA)
San Isabel National Forest Multiple Use Advisory Committee (USDA)
San Juan National Forest Multiple Use Advisory Committee (USDA)
San Juan Section, San Juan National Forest Grazing Advisory Board (USDA)

---

* Ten separate committees.

Santa Fe National Forest Grazing Advisory Board (USDA)
Sawtooth National Forest Grazing Advisory Board (USDA)
Sawtooth National Forest Multiple Use Advisory Committee (USDA)
Science Advisory Board—National Center for Toxicological Research
 (HEW)
Science Information Council (NSF)
Scientific Advisory Committee (DOD)
Scientific Advisory Group (DOD)
Scientific Advisory Group for the Joint Strategic Target Planning Staff
 (DOD)
Scientific Advisory Group on Effects (DOD)
Sea Grant Advisory Panel (DOC)
SecDef Natural Resources Conservation Award Selection Committee (DOD)
Secretary of State's Advisory Committee on Private International Law (DOS)
Secretary of the Navy's Advisory Board on Education and Training (DOD)
Secretary of the Navy's Advisory Committee on Naval History (DOD)
Secretary of the Navy's Audit Advisory Committee (DOD)
Secretary's Advisory Committee on Metal and Nonmetallic Mine Health and
 Safety (DOI)
Secretary's Advisory Committee on Population Affairs (HEW)
Secretary's Advisory Committee on Rights and Responsibilities of Women
 (HEW)
Securities Industry Association, Government Securities and Federal Agencies
 Committee (TRES)
Semiconductor Manufacturing and Test Equipment Technical Advisory
 Committee (DOC)
Semiconductor Technical Advisory Committee (DOC)
Senior Utility Steering Committee (AEC)
Senior Utility Technical Advisory Committee (AEC)
Ship Structure Committee (DOT)
Shippers' Advisory Committee (USDA)
Shipping Coordinating Committee (DOS)
Shoshone National Forest Advisory Committee (USDA)
Shoshone National Forest Livestock Advisory Board (USDA)
Sickel Cell Disease Advisory Committee (HEW)
Sitgreaves National Forest Grazing Advisory Board (USDA)
Sitgreaves National Forest Multiple Use Advisory Committee (USDA)
Siuslaw National Forest Advisory Committee (USDA)
Sleeping Bear Dunes National Lakeshore Advisory Commission (DOI)
Small Business Investment Company National Advisory Council (SBA)
Social Problems Research Review Committee (HEW)
Social Sciences Research Review Committee (HEW)
Solid Tumor Virus Working Group (HEW)
South Kaibab Grazing Advisory Board (USDA)
Southeastern Regional Manpower Advisory Committee (DOL)

Southwestern Regional Manpower Advisory Committee (DOL)
Space Program Advisory Council (SPAC) (NASA)
   Applications Committee
   Life Sciences Committee
   Physical Sciences Committee
   Space Systems Committee
Spearfish District Grazing Advisory Board, Black Hills National Forest
   (USDA)
Special Advisory Committee on the Papers of Blacks (GSA)
Special Advisory Committee on the Papers of Notable American Women
   (GSA)
Special Medical Advisory Group (VA)
Special Working Group on Hardness Assurance (DOD)
Spray Adhesives Ad Hoc Committee (CPSC)
Standards Advisory Committee on Agriculture (DOL)
Standards Advisory Committee on Heat Stress (DOL)
Standing State Advisory Committee of the Water Resources Council (WRC)
Stanislaus Forest-wide Livestock Advisory Board (USDA)
State Advisory Committees (separate committees, one for each
   state and the District of Columbia) (CCR)
State Multiple-Use Advisory Boards (11 each) (DOI)
Stemming and Closure Panel (DOD)
Superior National Forest Advisory Committee (USDA)
Surgery A Study Section (HEW)
Surgery B Study Section (HEW)
Surgical Drugs Advisory Committee (HEW)

Targhee National Forest Multiple Use Advisory Committee (USDA)
Task Force on Education and Training for Minority Business Enterprise
   (HEW)
Taso-Penasco-Questa Division Grazing Advisory Board, Carson National
   Forest (USDA)
Technical Advisory Committee on Poison Prevention Packaging (CPSC)
Technical Advisory Group for Municipal Waste Water Systems (EPA)
Technical Electronic Product Radiation Safety Standards Committee (HEW)
Technical Pipeline Safety Standards Committee (DOT)
Technical Subcommittee of the Advisory Committee on Explosives Tagging
   (TRES)
Telecommunications Equipment Technical Advisory Committee (DOC)
Theatre Advisory Panel (NEA)
Therapeutic Evaluations Committee (HEW)
Third National Cancer Survey Utilization Advisory Committee (HEW)
Thrombosis Advisory Committee (HEW)
Tierra Amarilla Division Grazing Advisory Board, Carson National Forest
   (USDA)

Timber and Watershed Management Research Advisory Committee (USDA)
Timpas Unit Grazing Advisory Board, San Isabel National Forest (USDA)
Tobacco Working Group (HEW)
Toiyabe National Forest Livestock Advisory Board—Mono Division (USDA)
Tokay Grapes Shippers' Advisory Committee (USDA)
Tonto National Forest Grazing Advisory Board (USDA)
Tonto National Forest Multiple Use Advisory Committee (USDA)
Toxicology Study Section (HEW)
Transplantation and Immunology Committee (HEW)
Travel Advisory Board (DOC)
Tropical Medicine and Parasitology Study Section (HEW)
Tuberculosis Control Advisory Committee (HEW)

Uinta National Forest Grazing Advisory Board (USDA)
Umatilla National Forest Grazing Advisory Board (USDA)
Union County Grazing Advisory Board, Cibola National Forest (USDA)
U.S. Advisory Commission on Information (USIA)
U.S. Advisory Commission on International Education and Cultural Affairs
    (DOS)
U.S. Advisory Committee on Obstacle Clearance Requirements (DOT)
U.S. Advisory Committee on Visual Aids to Approach and Landing (DOT)
U.S. Air Force Academy Fine Arts Committee (DOD)
USAF Scientific Advisory Board (DOD)
U.S. Army Armaments Command Scientific Advisory Group (DOD)
U.S. Army Aviation Systems Command Scientific Advisory Group (DOD)
U.S. Army Club Management Agency Advisory Committee (DOD)
U.S. Army Medical Research and Development (DOD)
U.S. Army Military History Research Collection Advisory Committee (DOD)
U.S. Army Missile Command Scientific Advisory Group (DOD)
U.S. Army Tank Automotive Command Scientific Advisory Group (DOD)
U.S. Army Troop Support Command Scientific Advisory Group (DOD)
U.S. CCIR National Committee (DOS)
    (International Radio Consultative Committee)
        Study Group 1   (Spectrum Utilization-Monitoring)
        Study Group 2   (Space Research & Radioastronomy Services)
        Study Group 3   (Fixed Service at Frequencies Below About 30 MH_z)
        Study Group 4   (Fixed Service Using Satellites)
        Study Group 5   (Propagation in Nonionized Media)
        Study Group 6   (Ionospheric Propagation)
        Study Group 7   (Standard-frequency & Time-signal Services)
        Study Group 8   (Mobile Services)
        Study Group 9   (Fixed Service Using Radio-Relay Systems)
        Study Group 10   (Broadcasting Service [Sound])
        Study Group 11   (Broadcasting Service [Television])

Study Group CMTT (C.C.I.R./C.C.I.T.T. Joint Study Group for
Television and Sound Transmission)
Study Group CMV (C.C.I.R./C.C.I.T.T. Joint Study Group on
Vocabulary)
U.S. CCITT National Committee (DOS)
(International Telegraph and Telephone Consultative Committee)
Study Group 1   (U.S. Government Regulatory Problems)
Study Group 2   (World and Regional Plan Committees)
Study Group 3   (Telegraph Operations)
Study Group 4   (Worldwide Telephone Network)
Study Group 5   (Data Transmission and New Data Networks)
U.S. Coast Guard Academy Advisory Committee (DOT)
U.S. Defense/Industry Advisory Group in Europe (DOD)
U.S. Military Academy Planning Advisory Board (DOD)
U.S. National Committee on Vital and Health Statistics (HEW)
U.S. Nuclear Data Committee (AEC)
U.S. Territorial Expansion Memorial Commission (DOI)

VA Actuarial Advisory Committee (VA)
Venereal Disease Control Advisory Committee (HEW)
Veterans Administration Voluntary Service National Advisory Committee
(VA)
Veterans Administration Wage Committee (VA)
Virology Study Section (HEW)
Vision Research Program Committee (HEW)
Visual Arts Advisory Panel (NEA)
Visual Sciences A Study Section (HEW)
Visual Sciences B Study Section (HEW)

Wallowa-Whitman National Forest Grazing Advisory Board (USDA)
Washington National Monument Society (DOI)
Wastach National Forest Advisory Committee (USDA)
Water Pollution Control Advisory Board (EPA)
Water Resources Research Advisory Panel (DOI)
Waterfowl Advisory Committee (DOI)
Western States Regional Manpower Advisory Committee (DOL)
White Mountain National Forest Advisory Committee (USDA)
White River National Forest Multiple Use Advisory Committee (USDA)
Willamette National Forest Advisory Committee (USDA)
Winema National Forest Grazing Advisory Board (USDA)
Winter Navigation Board (DOD)
Wolf Trap Farm Park Advisory Board (DOI)
Women's Advisory Committee on Aviation (DOT)

Youths Highway Safety Advisory Committee (DOT)

Index

204

Sagan, John, 97
San Diego Union, 142
Saunders, Ed, 67
Saxbe, William, 16
Scherle, Rep. William, 68
Schwarz, Walter, 163
Seidel, Frederick, 68, 69
Selective Service System, 36, 37, 145
Senate Appropriations Committee, 37,
    93, 134, 135
Senate Budget Committee, 17
Senate Foreign Relations Committee,
    96, 97, 160, 164
Senate Public Works Committee, 62
Shelling, Thomas, 164
Simon, William, 13, 18
Small Business Administration, 41-46
Smith, Chesterfield, 137
Smithsonian Institution, 71, 166-172
Social Problems Research Review
    Committee, 24
Social Security Administration, 145
Soviet Union, aid to, 117, 118, 120
Speaker, Fred, 111, 112
Standardization of Screw Threads,
    Commission on, 26
State, U.S. Department of, 145
Statistical Reporting Service, 151, 154
Status of Women, Interdepartmental
    Committee on the, 26
Straight, Michael, 69, 70
Strother, Robert S., 159, 160
Student Loan Marketing Association, 19
Symms, Rep. Steven, 122

Task Force on Women's Rights and
    Representatives, 26
Tax Foundation, Inc., 14
Telecommunications, Office of, 125, 126
Telephone revolving fund, 18
Theatre Advisory Panel, 24
Tillinghast, Charles, Jr., 116
Title V Commissions, 73n.
Trains Magazine, 50n.
Transportation, U.S. Department of, 31,
    63, 145, 147
Trans World Airlines (TWA), 55, 116

Treasury, U.S. Department of the, 16,
    167
Truman, President Harry S., 26

United Nations, 167n.
United States Board of Tea Appeals, 25
University of California, 25
Upper Great Lakes Regional
    Commission, 73-76
U.S. Botanic Garden, 139, 140
U.S. Chamber of Commerce, 14
U.S. Employment Service, 59
U.S. Government Organization Manual,
    58, 130, 131
U.S. Information Agency, 30-32
U.S. Office of Education, 71, 90, 133,
    134, 142
U.S. Railroad Administration, 51, 52

Vanik, Rep. Charles, 117
Veterans Administration, 31, 33
Virginia Electric Power Company, 44
Voice of America, 30

Wallace, Mike, 33-35
Wall Street Journal, 116, 120, 170
War on Poverty, 73
Washington, George, 23, 24
Washington Post, 69
Washington Star, 69
Waterfowl Advisory Committee, 24
Ways and Means Committee, U.S.
    House, 105
Weinberger, Caspar, 34, 35
Western Center on Law and Poverty,
    111
Whitehead, Clay T., 126
White House Office of Science and
    Technology, 63n.
White House Office of
    Telecommunications Policy, 29, 30,
    34, 125, 126